Our Lord has written the promise of resurrection, not in books alone, but in every leaf in springtime.

Martin Luther

Be true to yourself, help others, make each day your masterpiece, make friendship a fine art, drink deeply from good books - especially the Bible, build a shelter against a rainy day, give thanks for your blessings and pray for guidance every day.

John Wooden

Earth and sky, woods and fields, lakes and rivers, the mountain and the sea, are excellent schoolmasters, and teach some of us more than we can ever learn from books.

John Lubbock

The things I want to know are in books; my best friend is the man who'll get me a book I ain't read.

Abraham Lincoln

Good friends, good books and a sleepy conscience: this is

the ideal life.

Mark Twain

The books that help you most are those which make you
think that most. The hardest way of learning is that of easy
reading; but a great book that comes from a great thinker is
a ship of thought, deep freighted with truth and beauty.

Pablo Neruda

A morning-glory at my window satisfies me more than the
metaphysics of books.

Walt Whitman

The reading of all good books is like a conversation with
the finest minds of past centuries.

Rene Descartes

I wanted to escape Small Town U.S.A. To dismiss the
boundaries, to explore. My life experience came from
watching movies, TV, and reading books and magazines.
When your culture comes from watching TV everyday,
you're bombarded with images of things that seem cool,

places that seem interesting, people who have jobs and careers and opportunities.

Trent Reznor

We are the children of a technological age. We have found streamlined ways of doing much of our routine work. Printing is no longer the only way of reproducing books. Reading them, however, has not changed.

Lawrence Clark Powell

You don't have to burn books to destroy a culture. Just get people to stop reading them.

Ray Bradbury

I would never want a book's autograph. I am a proud non-reader of books.

Kanye West

There is more treasure in books than in all the pirate's loot on Treasure Island.

Walt Disney

And this, our life, exempt from public haunt, finds tongues in trees, books in the running brooks, sermons in stones, and good in everything.

William Shakespeare

Be true to yourself. Make each day a masterpiece. Help others. Drink deeply from good books. Make friendship a fine art. Build a shelter against a rainy day.

John Wooden

Be careful about reading health books. You may die of a misprint.

Mark Twain

Have you ever heard the expression: Walk a mile in my shoes, and then judge me? And write your own books.

Ann Rule

Reading about nature is fine, but if a person walks in the woods and listens carefully, he can learn more than what is in books, for they speak with the voice of God.

George Washington Carver

I love everything that's old, - old friends, old times, old manners, old books, old wine.

Oliver Goldsmith

Muslims are not bloodthirsty people. Islam is a religion of peace that forbids the killing of the innocent. Islam also accepts the Prophets, whether those prophets are Mohammed, God's peace and blessing be upon Him, or Moses or the other prophets of the Books.

Abdullah of Saudi Arabia

We have talked long enough in this country about equal rights. It is time now to write the next chapter - and to write it in the books of law.

Lyndon B. Johnson

When I was a child I devoured every book I could get my hands on. I loved losing myself in colourful and dramatic stories - and my absolute favourite was 'Charlie And The Chocolate Factory.' Everything about it electrified me, and when I re-read Roald Dahl's books as an adult it surprised

me.

David Walliams

If the First Amendment means anything, it means that a state has no business telling a man, sitting alone in his house, what books he may read or what films he may watch.

Thurgood Marshall

I still find each day too short for all the thoughts I want to think, all the walks I want to take, all the books I want to read, and all the friends I want to see.

John Burroughs

I was so inspired by Dr. King that in 1956, with some of my brothers and sisters and first cousins - I was only 16 years old - we went down to the public library trying to check out some books, and we were told by the librarian that the library was for whites only and not for colors. It was a public library.

John Lewis

To paint comic books as childish and illiterate is lazy. A lot of comic books are very literate - unlike most films.

Alan Moore

My attitudes have changed, but somebody would have to read all my books to find out how they have.

Irwin Shaw

When I was 10 years old, I loved - I loved books, and I used to haunt the secondhand bookshop. And I found a little book I could just afford, and I bought it, and I took it home. And I climbed up my favorite tree, and I read that book from cover to cover. And that was Tarzan of the Apes. I immediately fell in love with Tarzan.

Jane Goodall

Honorary degrees and lifetime achievement awards are very encouraging. I know that it might sound strange that a writer who has published many books still needs encouragement, but this is true.

Joyce Carol Oates

I've been reading Greek mythology since I was a kid. I also taught it when I was a sixth grade teacher, so I knew a lot of mythological monsters already. Sometimes I still use books and Web sites to research, though. Every time I research Greek mythology, I learn something new!

Rick Riordan

You've got all these books on self help, getting to know yourself, doing the right thing, eating the so-called right foods, even down to what books you have on your shelves. People are encouraged to look to themselves first as opposed to being a part of society.

Samantha Morton

I always wrote. I wrote from when I was 12. That was therapeutic for me in those days. I wrote things to get them out of feeling them, and onto paper. So writing in a way saved me, kept me company. I did the traditional thing with falling in love with words, reading books and underlining lines I liked and words I didn't know.

Carrie Fisher

In one of my recent books, 'The Success Principles,' I taught 64 lessons that help people achieve what they want out of life. From taking nothing less than 100 percent

responsibility for your life to empowering others, these are the fundamentals to success - and to great leadership.

Jack Canfield

Jews read the books of Moses not just as history but as divine command. The question to which they are an answer is not, 'What happened?' but rather, 'How then shall I live?' And it's only with the exodus that the life of the commands really begins.

Jonathan Sacks

There are two things that I cannot live without: music and books. Caffeine isn't dignified enough to qualify.

Carlos Ruiz Zafon

A recluse without books and ink is already in life a dead man.

Alfred Nobel

For me, books have always been a way to feel less alone while being alone. Perhaps if I was depressed and isolated, just communicating with these authors through their

sentences helped me.

Jonathan Ames

I would love to do a cookery show and cookery books. I'm not a professional cook, but I can definitely cook. I know the difference between good and bad cooking. I mean, when I was in 'Big Brother' I was the glorified cook of the house, so if I got offered my own show - then why not?

Shilpa Shetty

Many self-help books give you these neat, tidy formulas that are really illusions. They dupe people into thinking, 'Well if I can just do that, then everything's going to be okay.' My work differs in that I don't offer quick solutions and simple explanations.

John Bradshaw

There often is a dark secret in books... There is often a gathering sense of dread; there's a gap sometimes in the text from which all kinds of monsters can emerge.

Anne Enright

One of the things I'm trying to do over and over again in my books is create new mythologies, create new ways to understand the complexity of the world. I think what mythology does is impress upon chaotic experience the patterns, hierarchies and shapes which allow us to interpret the chaos and make fresh sense of it.

Clive Barker

For people like me, books are something solid and real, whereas digital stuff is a bit more ethereal. I like the trophy on my shelf, the presence in my home. A nice book is just as valuable as a decoration as a beautiful porcelain urn - and, let's face it, a hell of a lot more useful.

John Romaniello

I'm not actually sure I'm grown-up enough for grown-up books.

Barbara Park

The man who does not read good books has no advantage over the man who cannot read them.

Mark Twain

For a person who grew up in the '30s and '40s in the segregated South, with so many doors closed without explanation to me, libraries and books said, 'Here I am, read me.' Over time I have learned I am at my best around books.

Maya Angelou

My observations are not bread crumbs. They do not dissolve. They are on record, on film printed in books, and found on the Internet. I am happy to share them. For this I was born.

Bill Cosby

Books can only reveal us to ourselves, and as often as they do us this service we lay them aside.

Henry David Thoreau

The instruction we find in books is like fire. We fetch it from our neighbours, kindle it at home, communicate it to others, and it becomes the property of all.

Voltaire

Books, like friends, should be few and well chosen. Like friends, too, we should return to them again and again for, like true friends, they will never fail us - never cease to instruct - never cloy.

Charles Caleb Colton

The best books... are those that tell you what you know already.

George Orwell

When I get a little money I buy books; and if any is left I buy food and clothes.

Desiderius Erasmus

And they write innumerable books; being too vain and distracted for silence: seeking every one after his own elevation, and dodging his emptiness.

T. S. Eliot

Some books are to be tasted, others to be swallowed, and some few to be chewed and digested.

Francis Bacon

One person who has mastered life is better than a thousand persons who have mastered only the contents of books, but no one can get anything out of life without God.

Meister Eckhart

The Koran shows every sign of being thrown together by human beings, as do all the other holy books.

Christopher Hitchens

Mum had done everything you need to educate a kid. She made me a kid who likes books and she told me about 'Wind in the Willows' and read it and I thought this is weird, Rat, Mole, Toad and my first ever Bolshie thought - you know about 'The Wind in the Willows.'

Terry Pratchett

It is much simpler to buy books than to read them and easier to read them than to absorb their contents.

William Osler

Books have the same enemies as people: fire, humidity,

animals, weather, and their own content.

Paul Valery

Deep-versed in books and shallow in himself.

John Milton

The one thing I regret is that I will never have time to read all the books I want to read.

Francoise Sagan

Who knows for what we live, and struggle, and die? Wise men write many books, in words too hard to understand. But this, the purpose of our lives, the end of all our struggle, is beyond all human wisdom.

Alan Paton

A book is a fragile creature, it suffers the wear of time, it fears rodents, the elements and clumsy hands. so the librarian protects the books not only against mankind but also against nature and devotes his life to this war with the forces of oblivion.

Umberto Eco

In the case of good books, the point is not to see how many of them you can get through, but how many can get through to you.

Mortimer Adler

With a few flowers in my garden, half a dozen pictures and some books, I live without envy.

Lope de Vega

My own experience with being interviewed is mixed. I suppose they're a part of my job, and as I would like readers to connect with my books, I do them. I've also made many lifelong friends whom I first encountered as interviewers - as a writer, they're a terrific way to meet and add smart new people to one's life.

Douglas Coupland

I try to write the books I would love to come upon that are honest, concerned with real lives, human hearts, spiritual transformation, families, secrets, wonder, craziness - and that can make me laugh.

Anne Lamott

I found that the recipes in most - in all - the books I had were really not adequate. They didn't tell you enough... I won't do anything unless I'm told why I'm doing it. So I felt that we needed fuller explanations so that if you followed one of those recipes, it should turn out exactly right.

Julia Child

Books are challenging and inspirational to me.

Amy Sedaris

The books that help you the most are those which make you think the most.

Theodore Parker

The power of a book lies in its power to turn a solitary act into a shared vision. As long as we have books, we are not alone.

Laura Bush

The idea that a book can advise a woman how to capture a man is touchingly naive. Books advising men how to

capture a woman are far less common, perhaps because few men are willing to admit to such a difficulty. For both sexes, I recommend a good novel, offering scenarios you might learn from, if only because they reflect a lot of doubt.

Roger Ebert

You cannot write for children They're much too complicated. You can only write books that are of interest to them.

Maurice Sendak

I've written 18 books, mostly dealing with issues of social justice, ending racism, feminism, and cultural criticism.

bell hooks

Books have led some to learning and others to madness.

Petrarch

If you feel that there's the author and then the character, then the book is not working. People have a habit of identifying the author with the narrator, and you can't, obviously, be all of the narrators in all of your books, or

else you'd be a very strange person indeed.

Margaret Atwood

I'm so excited. I love Peeta so much. I think that over the course of the next couple of books, he has so many interesting places to go to, character-wise. I'm ready to dive full-force into it. When I saw the movie actually, it got me energized. 'Let's go get some cameras! Let's go shoot the second one right now!'

Josh Hutcherson

'Ageism,' or whatever you want to call it, is a very English phenomenon. You don't get it too much in many other cultures. And no one says it about authors or poets or filmmakers. 'Oh, they're too old to make films or write books.'

Paul Weller

Access to books and the encouragement of the habit of reading: these two things are the first and most necessary steps in education and librarians, teachers and parents all over the country know it. It is our children's right and it is also our best hope and their best hope for the future.

Michael Morpurgo

I sort of try to read the books when they come out impartially and not make up my mind, but the fact is when I was reading the sixth, 'Harry Potter And The Half-Blood Prince', there were bits in there where I was going, 'God, I would love to do that because it's so good'.

Daniel Radcliffe

I'm kind of old-school and love nothing more than sitting, opening a book, and reading it. But I also love listening to audio books.

Nick Cave

One of the nice things about books as opposed to television and movies to some extent is it's not a passive entertainment. People really do get involved, and they do create, and they do have their own visions of what different characters look like and what should happen. It's great - it means their brains are working.

James Patterson

Another hero was Tom Swift, in the books. What he stood for, the freedom, the scientific knowledge and being and engineer gave him the ability to invent solutions to

problems. He's always been a hero to me. I buy old Tom Swift books now and read them to my own children.

Steve Wozniak

I have said repeatedly that in this country we track library books better than we do sex offenders.

Mark Foley

I've got a vendetta to destroy the Net, to make everyone go to the library. I love the organic thing of pen and paper, ink on canvas. I love going down to the library, the feel and smell of books.

Joseph Fiennes

Catch me on a good day, I think half of my books aren't too bad. Catch me on a bad day, I think I've never written a good line.

Dennis Lehane

The ecological impact of book manufacture and traditional book marketing - I think that should really be considered. We have this industry in which we cut down trees to make

the paper that we then use enormous amounts of electricity to turn into books that weigh a great deal and are then shipped enormous distances to point-of-sale retail.

William Gibson

My family put a lot of emphasis on homework, so there weren't too many comic books or video games for me, when I was growing up.

Wentworth Miller

My perfect reader doesn't just read - he or she devours books.

Anthony Horowitz

Of all the ways of acquiring books, writing them oneself is regarded as the most praiseworthy method. Writers are really people who write books not because they are poor, but because they are dissatisfied with the books which they could buy but do not like.

Walter Benjamin

In Chinese culture, it wouldn't occur to kids to question or

talk back to their parents. In American culture, kids in books, TV shows and movies constantly score points with their snappy back talk. Typically, it's the parents who need to be taught a life lesson - by their children.

Amy Chua

I organize a chess festival in Hungary. I support chess in schools, and I have my own chess foundation. And I started writing books.

Garry Kasparov

I think it's difficult for young people to acknowledge being smart, to knowledge being a reader. I see kids who are embarrassed to read books. They're embarrassed to have people see them doing it.

Walter Dean Myers

When I was 13 or 14, my mother used to gift me books that I was dying to read. Those are my most memorable birthday gifts.

Kajol

My mother always kept library books in the house, and one rainy Sunday afternoon - this was before television, and we didn't even have a radio - I picked up a book to look at the pictures and discovered I was reading and enjoying what I read.

Beverly Cleary

I like to build places online where readers can have productive conversations about books.

John Green

Adventure books are my personal favorites. 'The Endurance,' a story about Ernest Shackleton's legendary Antarctica expedition, or 'Into Thin Air,' Jon Krakauer's personal account of the 1996 disaster on Mt Everest, are two notables.

Dean Karnazes

The old Victorian laws against homosexuality were still on the statute books until the early 1990s. As a gay man living in Ireland, I and people like me found it easy to feel less than citizens.

Colm Toibin

My father was sleepless most of his life. So by the age of five, I was awake with him all night long, watching bad television or we'd lie in the same bed, and I'd read my comic books while he read his latest spy or mystery novel.

Sherman Alexie

My son craves picture books about Transformers and Ninja Turtles and the Hulk; they show one fantastic creature smashing or zapping another into smithereens on page after page. They are dull and ugly and show no interesting stories or models of conflict resolution or character building.

Russell Smith

I think the advent of the Internet gave us all a big boost, because by the time the Internet became mainstream and you could get it in your home, a lot of us were used to dealing in fan culture, writing to magazines or anything at the back of comic books.

Kevin Smith

'Just looking at pictures' used to be considered cheating. No longer. The graphic novel is booming. Comics, heavily

illustrated texts, books with no words are now accepted as reading.

Jon Scieszka

On my first days here I did not start work immediately but, as planned, I took it easy for a few days - flicked through books, studied Japanese art a little.

Gustav Klimt

I don't like Communism because it hands out wealth through rationing books.

Omar Torrijos Herrera

Many of the books I loved as a kid, that even my mother read as a child, are very slow going. Today's children are not as patient. The best example of this is 'The Secret Garden,' which I adored as a child.

Lois Lowry

Pretending that there are no choices to be made - reading only books, for example, which are cheery and safe and nice - is a prescription for disaster for the young.

Lois Lowry

All books are either dreams or swords, you can cut, or you can drug, with words.

Amy Lowell

Lines that are funny don't make me laugh until years later. Before I write something new, I'll usually pick up one of my books, doesn't matter which one, and start reading it to get into the rhythm of the prose. I'll be in a scene and hear these people talk, and someone says something and I'll laugh out loud - which I didn't at the time I wrote it.

Elmore Leonard

I wrote 'Yellow Submarine' for the Beatles. I wrote the screenplay for 'The Games,' about the Olympic Games. I wrote 'Love Story,' both the novel and the screenplay. I wrote 'RPM' for Stanley Kramer. Plus, I wrote two scholarly books and a 400-page translation from the Latin, and I dated June Wilkinson!

Erich Segal

There are two books that I often travel with; one is 'The

Theory on Moral Sentiments' by Adam Smith. The other is 'The Meditations.' It's not that I agree with either views expressed in the books, but I believe ideas and thoughts of older generations can offer food for thought for the current generation.

Wen Jiabao

Through the eight books in 'The Treasure Chest' series, readers will meet twins Maisie and Felix and learn the secrets and rules of time travel, where they will encounter some of these famous and forgotten people. In Book 1, Clara Barton, then Alexander Hamilton, Pearl Buck, Harry Houdini, and on and on.

Ann Hood

I'm the only girl on The Food Network who grills - I have two bestselling grilling books. I try to really focus on what men and women can do outside together out on the grill. I think it's really fun to have men and women out there together, having fun, working and enjoying themselves.

Sandra Lee

You have to take your ego out of it and say, do I want people to be obsequious to me or do I want to write good books? If it's the latter, you have to take criticism. It's

annoying, but that's how to do good stuff; listen to other people.

Denise Mina

I believe in books that do not go to a ready-made public. I'm looking for readers I would like to make. To win them, to create readers rather than to give something that readers are expecting. That would bore me to death.

Carlos Fuentes

We live in a dark time. Books are as dark as what is available to teenagers through the media every day.

Tamora Pierce

I didn't like books where people played on a sports team and won a bunch of games, or went to summer camp and had a wonderful time. I really liked a book where a witch might cut a child's head off or a pack of angry dogs might burst through a door and terrorize a family.

Daniel Handler

I'm one of those freaky people that actually reads books.

Jason Momoa

My parents took an interest in nothing, at home no books, no records. My mother and my father are the emblem of indifference, dryness and bad taste. My father is also terribly stingy, in life as well as in feelings: I have never seen him filling up the bathtub.

Vincent Gallo

Once I start reading something, I can't stop. I obsessively read, which is a problem with long books!

Keegan Allen

I love the fact that so many of my readers are intelligent, exceptional, accomplished people with an open-minded love of diversity. But even more than that, I love it when my readers find lasting friendship with others of my readers - knowing that they met through their mutual affection for my books and characters makes me happy!

Suzanne Brockmann

Before I left the 'Star' last year to write books full-time, I welcomed catastrophe. It was material. Missed planes,

broken pipes, dead lawns, digestive disorders, you name it, if it was something that had gone horribly wrong, it was worth banging out 600 words about.

Linwood Barclay

I loved to read when I was a kid, and as soon as I realized that an actual person got to make up the books I loved so much, I decided that that was the job for me.

Margaret Haddix

I always have been and will remain someone who loves real, 3D, substantial books. And I don't believe that it's a wistful, nostalgic interest like vinyl collectors. It's not the same thing.

Art Spiegelman

There is no such thing as a moral or an immoral book. Books are well written, or badly written.

Oscar Wilde

Each age, it is found, must write its own books; or rather, each generation for the next succeeding.

Ralph Waldo Emerson

Some books leave us free and some books make us free.

Ralph Waldo Emerson

Read the best books first, or you may not have a chance to read them at all.

Henry David Thoreau

Books are the treasured wealth of the world and the fit inheritance of generations and nations.

Henry David Thoreau

Books are to be distinguished by the grandeur of their topics even more than by the manner in which they are treated.

Henry David Thoreau

I read a lot of obscure books and it is nice to open a book.

Bill Gates

I am a writer of books in retrospect. I talk in order to understand; I teach in order to learn.

Robert Frost

For a highly motivated learner, it's not like knowledge is secret and somehow the Internet made it not secret. It just made knowledge easy to find. If you're a motivated enough learner, books are pretty good.

Bill Gates

The worst thing about new books is that they keep us from reading the old ones.

John Wooden

Books are good enough in their own way, but they are a poor substitute for life.

Robert Louis Stevenson

I don't mind saying, you know, that I don't take a salary from the church, and God has blessed me with more money than I could imagine from my books. It's been printed all

over, so I don't feel like I am hiding anything.

Joel Osteen

A room without books is like a body without a soul.

Gilbert K. Chesterton

To buy books would be a good thing if we also could buy the time to read them.

Arthur Schopenhauer

I wrote a few children's books... not on purpose.

Steven Wright

Meditation has been a loyal friend to me. It has helped me write my books.

Alice Walker

All that mankind has done, thought or been: it is lying as in magic preservation in the pages of books.

Thomas Carlyle

I am not a self-help writer. I am a self-problem writer. When people read my books, I provoke some things. I cannot justify my work. I do my work; it is up to them to classify it, to judge.

Paulo Coelho

I don't believe in personal immortality; the only way I expect to have some version of such a thing is through my books.

Isaac Asimov

I want my books sold on airport bookstalls.

Stephen Hawking

It was books that taught me that the things that tormented me most were the very things that connected me with all the people who were alive, or who had ever been alive.

James A. Baldwin

Books are alive, you see. They're not dead, they're alive.

Ray Bradbury

Books like friends, should be few and well-chosen.

Samuel Johnson

I'm not into fame. I'm not into making money, outside of financing my books. I'm not into status. My thing is basically about time - not wasting it.

Henry Rollins

An apology for the devil: it must be remembered that we have heard one side of the case. God has written all the books.

Samuel Butler

I hate books; they only teach us to talk about things we know nothing about.

Jean-Jacques Rousseau

Books are but waste paper unless we spend in action the wisdom we get from thought - asleep. When we are weary of the living, we may repair to the dead, who have nothing of peevishness, pride, or design in their conversation.

William Butler Yeats

The real purpose of books is to trap the mind into doing its own thinking.

Christopher Morley

Nine-tenths of the existing books are nonsense and the clever books are the refutation of that nonsense.

Benjamin Disraeli

It's a fact that more people watch television and get their information that way than read books. I find new technology and new ways of communication very exciting and would like to do more in this field.

Stephen Covey

My books didn't fit a marketing niche.

Chuck Palahniuk

My favorite books to give or get are short story collections. And always paperbacks because they are easy to carry as you travel.

Chuck Palahniuk

Mr. Arthur Ashe, he was good. I read some of his books. He knew about everything, but he was real quiet and didn't talk much. I never met him.

Mike Tyson

Songs won't save the planet, but neither will books or speeches.

Pete Seeger

I love story songs because I've always loved books.

Dolly Parton

What do we, as a nation, care about books? How much do you think we spend altogether on our libraries, public or private, as compared with what we spend on our horses?

John Ruskin

At night, when the curtains are drawn and the fire flickers, my books attain a collective dignity.

E. M. Forster

Books are the legacies that a great genius leaves to mankind, which are delivered down from generation to generation as presents to the posterity of those who are yet unborn.

Joseph Addison

Sometimes music, movies and books are the only things that let us feel like someone else feels like we do.

Marilyn Manson

Next to acquiring good friends, the best acquisition is that of good books.

Charles Caleb Colton

Books open your mind, broaden your mind, and strengthen

you as nothing else can.

William Feather

I love great journalism. I appreciate it. I love a good, you know, I love good news stories. I love great books. I love great articles. I appreciate them so much, and they've been part of my education as a woman.

Angelina Jolie

My personal theory is that younger audiences disdain books - not because those readers are dumber than past readers, but because today's reader is smarter.

Chuck Palahniuk

With a book, you're guaranteed the audience has a certain skill level and that the audience has to make an ongoing effort to consume this product and that the project is being consumed by just one person at a time. I really want to play to that strength because it's one of the few advantages books still have.

Chuck Palahniuk

Any kid who has two parents who are interested in him and has a houseful of books isn't poor.

Sam Levenson

I love the movies, and when I go to see a movie that's been made from one of my books, I know that it isn't going to be exactly like my novel because a lot of other people have interpreted it. But I also know it has an idea that I'll like because that idea occurred to me, and I spent a year, or a year and a half of my life working on it.

Stephen King

The first books I was interested in were all about baseball. But I can't think of one single book that changed my life in any way.

Charles Kuralt

In books, you can just wallow in dialogue, and you can just wallow in written words. In screenplays, every line has to serve the purpose of the line that's implied before it and the line that's implied after it. Maybe five lines have to do the work of fifty lines.

Chuck Palahniuk

I think Chris Brown gets kind of dismissed as a gay writer, and I think Chris's books are really, really smart. I wish his books sold a little more widely.

Chuck Palahniuk

The folks who read my books are so passionate about each one of them that the people making my movies are more afraid of my readership than they are of me.

Chuck Palahniuk

Books, the children of the brain.

Jonathan Swift

I knew I would read all kinds of books and try to get at what it is that makes good writers good. But I made no promises that I would write books a lot of people would like to read.

Carl Sandburg

I think it's more important to write something that brings men back to reading than it is to write for people who

already read. There's a reason men don't read, and it's because books don't serve men. It's time we produce books that serve men.

Chuck Palahniuk

Writing books is fun because after I do a show for a couple hours, I'm in a bus for 22 hours. It's not hard for me to look out the window and tell a joke here and there.

Willie Nelson

I've had all six of my books reach the New York Times bestseller list, which is especially rewarding seeing as I flunked out of high school twice because I couldn't write. It just goes to show you that we learn from our mistakes.

Robert Kiyosaki

If you read a lot of books, you're considered well-read. But if you watch a lot of TV, you're not considered well-viewed.

Lily Tomlin

The only books that influence us are those for which we are

ready, and which have gone a little farther down our particular path than we have yet got ourselves.

E. M. Forster

Some of the most famous books are the least worth reading. Their fame was due to their having done something that needed to be doing in their day. The work is done and the virtue of the book has expired.

Moliere

If a secret history of books could be written, and the author's private thoughts and meanings noted down alongside of his story, how many insipid volumes would become interesting, and dull tales excite the reader!

William Makepeace Thackeray

I had a friend who worked at a hospice, and he said people in their final moments don't discuss their successes, awards or what books they wrote or what they accomplished. They only talk about their loves and their regrets, and I think that's very telling.

Brad Pitt

Books and all forms of writing are terror to those who wish to suppress the truth.

Wole Soyinka

I don't think about who the audience is for my books.

J. K. Rowling

I would always want printed books.

J. K. Rowling

If the government ever imposes a tax on books - and I wouldn't put it past them - I'm in dead trouble.

Terry Pratchett

I write books back to back, and I work very hard on them.

Terry Pratchett

I don't travel and tell stories, because that's not the way these days. But I write my books to be read aloud, and I think of myself in that oral tradition.

Louis L'Amour

It cannot be said often enough that science fiction as a genre is incredibly educational - and I'm speaking the written science fiction, not 'Star Trek.' Science fiction writers tend to fill their books if they're clever with little bits of interesting stuff and real stuff.

Terry Pratchett

That is sad until one recalls how many bad books the world may yet be spared because of the busyness of writers.

Gore Vidal

Some books are undeservedly forgotten; none are undeservedly remembered.

W. H. Auden

My own books drive themselves. I know roughly where a book is going to end, but essentially the story develops under my fingers. It's just a matter of joining the dots.

Terry Pratchett

Books! I dunno if I ever told you this, but books are the greatest gift one person can give another.

Bono

The truth is that I know very few novelists who have been satisfied with the adaptation of their books for the screen.

Gabriel Garcia Marquez

As far as I'm concerned, I'm a writer who's writing books, and therefore, I don't want to die. You'd miss the end of the book wouldn't you? You can't die with an unfinished book.

Terry Pratchett

A bad book is the worse that it cannot repent. It has not been the devil's policy to keep the masses of mankind in ignorance; but finding that they will read, he is doing all in his power to poison their books.

John Kenneth Galbraith

I think I work much harder on the children's books. I suppose I enjoy that. I find it interesting that although there are more than 30 books in the Discworld series, it is the

four that were written for children which have won the awards. I've never been quite certain why this is.

Terry Pratchett

I want Books and Babies and Beef stews.

Sylvia Plath

Old books that have ceased to be of service should no more be abandoned than should old friends who have ceased to give pleasure.

Bernard Baruch

There is a soak-the-rich attitude in the air, a feeling that if you have a lot of money you must have got it by some ghastly means. I can quite happily say there was never any family money. All the money we got was mine, just from writing books.

Terry Pratchett

I don't read books much.

LeBron James

If children are studying the 20th century, I'm in their text books.

Paul McCartney

And if you are a parent, introduce your children to their neighborhood library. It will give them a real sense of independence to have their own library card and enjoy borrowing books.

Sarah Jessica Parker

I am not in the business of suppressing books.

Salman Rushdie

Nobody wants to read about the honest lawyer down the street who does real estate loans and wills. If you want to sell books, you have to write about the interesting lawyers - the guys who steal all the money and take off. That's the fun stuff.

John Grisham

It is chiefly through books that we enjoy intercourse with

superior minds. In the best books, great men talk to us, give us their most precious thoughts, and pour their souls into ours.

William Ellery Channing

When I was 7, my proudest possession would have been my bookshelf 'cause I had alphabetized all of the books on my bookshelf.

Neil Gaiman

The most accomplished way of using books is to serve them as some people do lords; learn their titles and then brag of their acquaintance.

Laurence Sterne

I've always been a homemaker, like, I like creating spaces. Even if I stay in a hotel, I'll unpack, I'll put my books out, I'll put my camera out, I'll throw a sweater over the lamp to get better light. I am a homemaker.

Drew Barrymore

I was one those kids who had books on them. Before

weddings, Bar Mitzvahs, funerals and anything else where you're actually meant to not be reading, my family would frisk me and take the book away. If they didn't find it by this point in the procedure, I would be sitting over in that corner completely unnoticed just reading my book.

Neil Gaiman

Faulkner is a writer who has had much to do with my soul, but Hemingway is the one who had the most to do with my craft - not simply for his books, but for his astounding knowledge of the aspect of craftsmanship in the science of writing.

Gabriel Garcia Marquez

I'm obsessed with zombies. I like watching zombie movies and I read zombie books.

Kevin Bacon

I look at my books the way parents look at their children. The fact that one becomes more successful than the others doesn't make me love the less successful one any less.

Alex Haley

The true treasure lies within. It is the underlying theme of the songs we sing, the shows we watch and the books we read. It is woven into the Psalms of the Bible, the ballads of the Beatles and practically every Bollywood film ever made. What is that treasure? Love. Love is the nature of the Divine.

Radhanath Swami

You could say, in a vulgar Freudian way, that I am the unhappy child who escapes into books. Even as a child, I was most happy being alone. This has not changed.

Slavoj Zizek

What I've always tried to find in my books are points at which the private lives of the characters, and also my own, intersect with the public life of the culture.

Salman Rushdie

Books are like a mirror. If an ass looks in, you can't expect an angel to look out.

B. C. Forbes

Books always help.

Aung San Suu Kyi

' The Lucky One' is at its heart a romance novel, elevated however by Nicholas Sparks' persuasive storytelling. Readers don't read his books because they're true, but because they ought to be true.

Roger Ebert

'American Gods' was designed to be, if not open-ended, at least a trilogy kind of shape, so there's definitely one more book, probably another couple of books there to get written.

Neil Gaiman

I had started to feel that somewhere in the second half of the 20th century, the idea of page-turning as a good thing had been lost. You were getting books that were the equivalent of absolutely beautifully prepared dishes of food that didn't taste like anything much.

Neil Gaiman

When I read James Joyce, I'm not really interested in the Dublin of 1904. I'm interested in being in the presence of a voice and a sensibility underpinned by an authenticity which, I think, if you're a good writer, you can extract from the specific details of your own time. I think most writers do hope that their books will be read in ten years.

Joseph O'Neill

We found nothing grand in the history of the Jews nor in the morals inculcated in the Pentateuch. I know of no other books that so fully teach the subjection and degradation of woman.

Elizabeth Cady Stanton

To me, reading a fashion magazine is the last thing I need to do. I've got books I need to read.

Vivienne Westwood

The best books for a man are not always those which the wise recommend, but often those which meet the peculiar wants, the natural thirst of his mind, and therefore awaken interest and rivet thought.

William Ellery Channing

We don't need lists of rights and wrongs, tables of do's and don'ts: we need books, time, and silence. Thou shalt not is soon forgotten, but Once upon a time lasts forever.

Philip Pullman

If God had meant Harvard professors to appear in People magazine, She wouldn't have invented The New York Review of Books.

Anna Quindlen

My favorite books, art pieces, films, and music, always have something jarring about them.

Pink

I find that the history books that we teach our kids with are not fully truthful, in my opinion.

Jesse Ventura

It may come as a surprise to people, but I'm actually quite boring and normal. What do I do? I read books. I drive my kid to school. I have lunch with my wife. I pick my kid up

from school. I go home.

Nicolas Cage

I would only read the novels that people classify as 'beach books' if I were being held prisoner and the only alternative was the 'Book of Mormon.'

Tom Robbins

If you want to read about love and marriage, you've got to buy two separate books.

Alan King

I would not ever try to be a show intellectual, which I was accused of doing a while on ABC. I thought you were supposed to read the guests' books.

Dick Cavett

I confess that I am a messy, disorganized and impatient reader: if the book doesn't grab me in the first 40 pages, I abandon it. I have piles of half-read books waiting for me to get acute hepatitis or some other serious condition that would force me to rest so that I could read more.

Isabel Allende

These days, there are many people around the world who listen to the songs that made me infamous and read the books that made me respectable.

Kinky Friedman

I do give books as gifts sometimes, when people would rather have one than a new Ferrari.

Dean Koontz

Quite simply, federal laws already on the books aimed at stopping the flow of illegal immigration must be enforced. Furthermore, states must be given the resources necessary to confront the problem, which includes strengthening the border patrol.

Allen West

I have given up reading books; I find it takes my mind off myself.

Oscar Levant

I always used to look at books and wonder how anybody could come up with so many words. But my divorce and then falling in love with somebody else has released in me an ability to write in other ways apart from songs.

Roger Waters

The experience gathered from books, though often valuable, is but the nature of learning; whereas the experience gained from actual life is one of the nature of wisdom.

Samuel Smiles

I love fiction because in fiction you go into the thoughts of people, the little people, the people who were defeated, the poor, the women, the children that are never in history books.

Isabel Allende

I've always loved words. I ate up all the books I could get my hands on, and when I couldn't get books, I read candy wrappers and labels on cereal and toothpaste boxes.

Judy Holliday

Each of my books is different. Deliberately... I wanted to create my society, my people, in their fullness.

Chinua Achebe

I've always had great respect for Paddington because he is amusingly English and eccentric. He is a great British institution and my generation grew up with the books and then Michael Horden's animations.

Stephen Fry

I don't read thrillers, romance or mystery, and I don't read self-help books because I don't believe in shortcuts and loopholes.

Isabel Allende

I was drawn to boxing because I got beat up as a kid. I was the kid with the piano books in a New York neighbourhood.

Billy Joel

I like to read in the dark. I like to go into the bathtub, turn out all the lights, and in the dark, read my books.

Penn Jillette

As an adolescent I wrote comic books, because I read lots of them, and fantasy novels set in Malaysia and Central Africa.

Umberto Eco

The wise man reads both books and life itself.

Lin Yutang

I get letters from college kids who have read Percy Jackson when they were younger who tell me, 'I just passed my Classics exam.' The books are accurate enough that they can serve as a gateway to Homer and Virgil.

Rick Riordan

To be an artist, you don't have to compose music or paint or be in the movies or write books. It's just a way of living. It has to do with paying attention, remembering, filtering what you see and answering back, participating in life.

Viggo Mortensen

More people should read books. It's the most concentrated experience you can have.

Vivienne Westwood

What a word is truth. Slippery, tricky, unreliable. I tried in these books to tell the truth.

Lillian Hellman

When I am dead, I hope it may be said: His sins were scarlet, but his books were read.

Hilaire Belloc

I think that the online world has actually brought books back. People are reading because they're reading the damn screen. That's more reading than people used to do.

Bill Murray

Who ever converses among old books will be hard to please among the new.

William Temple

If sex is such a natural phenomenon, how come there are so many books on how to do it?

Bette Midler

Keeping books on social aid is capitalistic nonsense. I just use the money for the poor. I can't stop to count it.

Evita Peron

I read on my iPad when I travel. I listen to audiobooks in the car. I read books in my bedroom, where I have a comfortable couch, a lamp and two dogs to keep me warm.

Isabel Allende

The difference between people who believe they have books inside of them and those who actually write books is sheer cussed persistence - the ability to make yourself work at your craft, every day - the belief, even in the face of obstacles, that you've got something worth saying.

Jennifer Weiner

I don't want to sound pretentious, but I love art, I like to go to museums, and I like to read books.

Rainn Wilson

During the 1980s, when Japan's economy was roaring and people were writing books with titles like 'Japan is Number One,' most Japanese college students didn't make the effort to become fluent in English.

Rebecca MacKinnon

I was a total education geek. I loved school. I loved learning. I loved doing homework. All of my books and notebooks from high school are underlined and highlighted and there are notes all over the margins. And you know, I was a theater kid too. I was all over the place.

Sophia Bush

My maternal grandmother - she was a compulsive reader. She had only been through five grades of elementary school, but she was a member of the municipal library, and she brought home two or three books a week for me. They could be dime novels or Balzac.

Umberto Eco

The reason I wrote political satire was because I thought it -

politics - was important... that public policy was important. Then I transitioned into books, then into radio.

Al Franken

When I was growing up, I was the most pretentious person I have ever met. I only read obscure books and watched obscure movies and only listened to obscure music.

Moby

Professional reviewers read so many bad books in the course of duty that they get an unhealthy craving for arresting phrases.

Evelyn Waugh

The odd thing about being a writer is you do tend to lose yourself in your books. Sometimes it seems like real life is flickering by and you're hardly a part of it. You remember the events in your books better than you remember the events that actually took place when you were writing them.

George R. R. Martin

With each book I write, I become more and more convinced that the books have a life of their own, quite apart from me.

Madeleine L'Engle

I guess my guilty pleasure would be listening to the British audio versions of the 'Harry Potter' books.

David Sedaris

You get to relive your childhood when you have a baby and you see these toys and these books you read when you were little - the innocence that you are able to maintain because you have to find that again in order to connect with your child keeps you in a special state of mind.

Idina Menzel

I live alone, with cats, books, pictures, fresh vegetables to cook, the garden, the hens to feed.

Jeanette Winterson

Mark Twain was a great traveler and he wrote three or four great travel books. I wouldn't say that I'm a travel novelist

but rather a novelist who travels - and who uses travel as a background for finding stories of places.

Paul Theroux

All the information you could want is constantly streaming at you like a runaway truck - books, newspaper stories, Web sites, apps, how-to videos, this article you're reading, even entire magazines devoted to single subjects like charcuterie or wedding cakes or pickles.

Mario Batali

I'm calling my book series the 'with God series.' And this next 'with God' book is Friendship with God, which comes out in November. This books challenges us to bring about the end of 'better' on this planet.

Neale Donald Walsch

I do not write for this generation. I am writing for other ages. If this could read me, they would burn my books, the work of my whole life. On the other hand, the generation which interprets these writings will be an educated generation; they will understand me and say: 'Not all were asleep in the nighttime of our grandparents.'

Jose Rizal

The best way to obtain truth and wisdom is not to ask from books, but to go to God in prayer, and obtain divine teaching.

Joseph Smith, Jr.

Good books, like good friends, are few and chosen; the more select, the more enjoyable.

Louisa May Alcott

When you have mastered numbers, you will in fact no longer be reading numbers, any more than you read words when reading books You will be reading meanings.

W. E. B. Du Bois

You can only learn so much from books. You can only learn so much from education. Ultimately, it is the wisdom of God that will carry you through in the toughest situations of life.

Ravi Zacharias

Study how water flows in a valley stream, smoothly and

freely between the rocks. Also learn from holy books and wise people. Everything - even mountains, rivers, plants and trees - should be your teacher.

Morihei Ueshiba

I talk to my readers on social networking sites, but I never tell them what the book is about. Writing is lonely, so from time to time I talk to them on the Internet. It's like chatting at a bar without leaving your office. I talk with them about a lot of things other than my books.

Paulo Coelho

He who studies medicine without books sails an uncharted sea, but he who studies medicine without patients does not go to sea at all.

William Osler

The love of learning, the sequestered nooks, And all the sweet serenity of books.

Henry Wadsworth Longfellow

Do not consider it proof just because it is written in books,

for a liar who will deceive with his tongue will not hesitate to do the same with his pen.

Maimonides

When I was a boy, I always saw myself as a hero in comic books and in movies. I grew up believing this dream.

Elvis Presley

Reading is a conversation. All books talk. But a good book listens as well.

Mark Haddon

To read too many books is harmful.

Mao Zedong

There are no makeovers in my books. The ugly duckling does not become a beautiful swan. She becomes a confident duck able to take charge of her own life and problems.

Maeve Binchy

The Bible and several other self help or enlightenment books cite the Seven Deadly Sins. They are: pride, greed, lust, envy, wrath, sloth, and gluttony. That pretty much covers everything that we do, that is sinful... or fun for that matter.

Dave Mustaine

If my books can help children become readers, then I feel I have accomplished something important.

Roald Dahl

Preachers in pulpits talked about what a great message is in the book. No matter what you do, somebody always imputes meaning into your books.

Dr. Seuss

All of the books in the world contain no more information than is broadcast as video in a single large American city in a single year. Not all bits have equal value.

Carl Sagan

When I was in prison, I was wrapped up in all those deep

books. That Tolstoy crap - people shouldn't read that stuff.

Mike Tyson

Wherever they burn books they will also, in the end, burn human beings.

Heinrich Heine

There are many little ways to enlarge your child's world. Love of books is the best of all.

Jackie Kennedy

I vowed to myself that when I grew up and became a theoretical physicist, in addition to doing research, I would write books that I would have liked to have read as a child. So whenever I write, I imagine myself, as a youth, reading my books, being thrilled by the incredible advances being made in physics and science.

Michio Kaku

I wish I had known that education is the key. That knowledge is power. Now I pick up books and watch educational shows with my husband. I'm seeing how

knowledge can elevate you.

Mary J. Blige

Let's face it: Most of us don't realize it, but we are failing our kids as reading role models. The best role models are in the home: brothers, fathers, grandfathers; mothers, sisters, grandmothers. Moms and dads, it's important that your kids see you reading. Not just books - reading the newspaper is good, too.

James Patterson

We shouldn't teach great books; we should teach a love of reading.

B. F. Skinner

There's books that are about places we will never go, and then there's books that inspire us to go.

Paul Theroux

If men were but to read the New Testament with the same tone and emphasis, with which they do other books, and were to keep out of mind the idea of its being sacred, they

would be disgusted with the credulity, and the want of intellect, reason and judgment, that is apparent in it.

Lysander Spooner

Self-improvement books, friends, and polite strangers often tell soothing lies about our physical appearance that prevent many of us from facing, discussing, and solving our real problems.

Martha Beck

I have piles of poetry books in the bathroom, on the stairs, everywhere. The only way to write poetry is to read it.

Carol Ann Duffy

It's sad when you can't make everyone happy, though. It's impossible but, at the same time, you still hope. You think, 'Maybe I can do it,' but you know you can't. But gosh, if I had to rely on giving people what they wanted, I would have had to write 40 billion different books and even then, I wouldn't get it right.

Stephenie Meyer

Christ himself wrote nothing, but furnished endless material for books and songs of gratitude and praise.

Philip Schaff

Literary imagination is an aesthetic object offered by a writer to a lover of books.

Gaston Bachelard

I want to spend my life with someone and do nice things and go on adventures, read books and have nice food and celebrate things. I don't want to spend the rest of my life in the bedroom like some people who just go to bed and never get out again.

Tracey Emin

Classics are books which, the more we think we know them through hearsay, the more original, unexpected, and innovative we find them when we actually read them.

Italo Calvino

Most people in America want an easy read. I call it McFiction - books which pass right through you without

you even digesting them. I don't mean a book that has two-syllable words. I mean chapters you can read in a toilet break. Happy endings. We are more of a TV culture.

Jodi Picoult

How some of the writers I come across get through their books without dying of boredom is beyond me.

William Gaddis

Focus in on the genre you want to write, and read books in that genre. A LOT of books by a variety of authors. And read with questions in your mind.

Nicholas Sparks

Live life and write about life. Of the making of many books there is indeed no end, but there are more than enough books about books.

Will Self

Perhaps it is partly that we need to love books ourselves as parents, grandparents and teachers in order to pass on that passion for stories to our children. It's not about testing and

reading schemes, but about loving stories and passing on that passion to our children.

Michael Morpurgo

Before I started chemotherapy treatments, I wrote down the best advice from doctors, family, friends, books, and survivors and created an 'Owner's Manual' to help me take care of myself. It would remind me that cancer is doable.

Regina Brett

When I was in the Peace Corps I never made a phone call. I was in Central Africa; I didn't make a phone call for two years. I was in Uganda for another four years and I didn't make a phone call. So for six years I didn't make a phone call, but I wrote letters, I wrote short stories, I wrote books.

Paul Theroux

If my books had been any worse, I should not have been invited to Hollywood, and if they had been any better, I should not have come.

Raymond Chandler

In my day, MI6 - which I called the Circus in the books - stank of wartime nostalgia. People were defined by secret cachet: one man did something absolutely extraordinary in Norway; another was the darling of the French Resistance. We didn't even show passes to go in and out of the building.

John le Carre

There are books on our shelves we haven't read and doubtless never will, that each of us has probably put to one side in the belief that we will read them later on, perhaps even in another life.

Umberto Eco

I always have several books on the go at any one moment, so it's no good you asking 'What's on the bedside table at the moment, Emma?' because often I can't even see the table!

Emma Watson

I think I'm a combination of very simple pleasures and the fact I've read a lot of books. I don't think it's a binary opposition across the board in humans and I think I'm an example that it's not. I'm hosting gay marriage rallies and I have tons of guns at home. There's a lot of middle ground

in the world and I'm one of those people.

Dax Shepard

I like nonfiction books about people with wretched lives.

David Sedaris

I'd never heard of the 'Lord of the Rings', actually. So I went to the bookstore and there it was, three shelves of books about Tolkien and Middle-earth, and I was like, 'Holy cow, what else am I missing out on?'

Sean Astin

The end of reading is not more books but more life.

Holbrook Jackson

I'm quite proud of what I anticipated about reality television from my books in the early '90s, which I based on the early seasons of 'Cops' and on the amazing stuff I had read about happening on Japanese shows and the British 'Big Brother'.

William Gibson

It's clear to me that there is no good reason for many philosophy books to sound as complicated as they do.

Alain de Botton

I like books that have razor-sharp plotting that snaps and moves along. It's not about the main character being different at the end. I don't want my main character to be different in the end. I still want him committed to his ideas, to be steadfast, true and loyal.

Brad Thor

When I wonder what the future of books will be, I often think about horses. Before automobiles existed, everyone had a horse. Then cars became available, and their convenience, compared to horses, was undeniable.

Susan Orlean

So we want an Islamic state where Islamic law is not just in the books but enforced, and enforced with determination. There is no space and no room for democratic consultation. The Shariah is set and fixed, so why do we need to discuss it anymore? Just implement it!

Abu Bakar Bashir

There are certain books in the world which every searcher for truth must know: the Bible, the Critique of Pure Reason, the Origin of Species, and Karl Marx's Capital.

Al Capp

I just love doing radio. I've learned to be more vulnerable through radio than even I've been through books and writing lyrics. It's a different type of experience where, if I'm writing a lyric, I can sort of hide behind it a little bit.

Nikki Sixx

Oftentimes I deliberately put ambiguity into my books so that... the reader is left with an echo of: 'How much of this was from me?'

Mohsin Hamid

I like to read books and be alone; I'm not social butterfly person. I'm sorry.

Hope Solo

My parents both had Oxford degrees, they read important books, spoke foreign languages, drank real coffee and went to museums for pleasure. People like that don't have fat kids: they were cut out to be winners and winners don't have children who are overweight.

Arabella Weir

The Twist was a guided missile launched from the ghetto into the heart of suburbia. The Twist succeeded, as politics, religion and law could never do, in writing in the heart and soul what the Supreme Court could only write on the books.

Eldridge Cleaver

I grew up reading 'Sense and Sensibility' and 'Pride and Prejudice' - girly kind of books.

Leighton Meester

It's always hard when you're playing someone for a lot of people out there who are going to see the movie after reading the books. There's a communion between a reader and the writer, so people will have an idea who Sirius Black is and I might not be everyone's idea of that.

Gary Oldman

Books and movies are different art forms with different rules. And because of that, they never translate exactly.

Tom Clancy

There's something about the air and the sky and the atmosphere in the South of France that must be very conducive to work, to being creative, because I have written several of my books there. I find it so much easier because you're cut off. If you don't want to speak to anybody, basically they don't know where you are. And it's so beautiful.

Joan Collins

How much energy is wasted in Italy in trying to write the novel that obeys all the rules. The energy might have been useful to provide us with more modest, more genuine things, that had less pretensions: short stories, memoirs, notes, testimonials, or at any rate, books that are open, without a preconceived plan.

Italo Calvino

The part of my writing I find the most rewarding is when people write to me or speak to me in public to tell me how

his or her life has been changed by my books.

Sidney Sheldon

In the last 1,000 years, the Arabs have translated as many books as Spain translates in just one year.

Larry Elder

When I was 12 years old, I read 'Nancy Drew' mysteries and biographies of Madame Curie and Florence Nightingale and books about girls who love horses or go to nursing school. I belonged to the Girl Scouts and got A's in school and rarely disobeyed my parents. I still kept a collection of Barbie dolls in my room, and I almost never spoke to boys.

Joyce Maynard

Don't patronize the chain bookstores. Every time I see some author scheduled to read and sign his books at a chain bookstore, I feel like telling him he's stabbing the independent bookstores in the back.

Lawrence Ferlinghetti

I got my love of animals from the Dr. Doolittle books and my love of Africa from the Tarzan novels. I remember my mum taking me to the first Tarzan film, which starred Johnny Weissmuller, and bursting into tears. It wasn't what I had imagined at all.

Jane Goodall

If I'm riding my bike I just replay the same scenarios over and over in my head, like I haven't had a new mental adventure since high school. So that's what I like about books on tape, so my mind can't wander anywhere.

David Sedaris

I started writing while I was a little boy. Maybe it's because I was reading a lot of books I admired, and thought that I would like to write something like that someday. Also, my love for good writing pushed me.

Naguib Mahfouz

I have expressed my opinion through the written word through my books, that is all.

Oriana Fallaci

Some people play the piano, some do Sudoku, some watch television, some people go out to dinner parties. I write books.

Boris Johnson

I don't care where I live, so long as there's a roof to keep the rain off my books, and high-speed Internet access.

Eliezer Yudkowsky

I would rather be poor in a cottage full of books than a king without the desire to read.

Thomas Babington Macaulay

I did the traditional thing with falling in love with words, reading books and underlining lines I liked and words I didn't know. It was something I always did.

Carrie Fisher

Books are standing counselors and preachers, always at hand, and always disinterested; having this advantage over oral instructors, that they are ready to repeat their lesson as often as we please.

Louis Nizer

The reason why so few good books are written is that so few people who can write know anything.

Walter Bagehot

I myself don't know what makes my books work. I enter a bookstore and I'm frankly overwhelmed by the number of books in most of them, and I know people are buying mine.

Chetan Bhagat

When I go on holiday and people ask me what I do, I tell them I do some internet stuff and I've done a couple of books and I hope they just leave it at that.

Karl Pilkington

We are as liable to be corrupted by books, as by companions.

Henry Fielding

Normally I would not recommend a book that tells you how

to make money in the stock market. Most of these books are aimed at gullible folk, and they usually make much more money for their authors than they do for the investing public.

Gavyn Davies

I like books that expose me to people unlike me and books that do battle against caricature or simplification. That, to me, is the heroic in fiction.

Zadie Smith

Anybody who can afford a box of business cards can afford a Web site. Any company with an 800 number can move its services to the Web for peanuts by comparison. The extreme case of corporate promotion is to strip away all other aspects of your business and sell goods or services via the Net alone, as amazon.com has done with books.

Nathan Myhrvold

When I was about nine years old, I announced to my mother that I was going to cook Thanksgiving dinner. And I went to the library and got this whole pile of books. I'd love to say it all turned out great. It didn't. But, sort of, from that point on, whenever there was serious cooking at home, I was the one who did it.

Nathan Myhrvold

I've never turned into a bee - I've never been chased by a mummy or met a ghost. But many of the ideas in my books are suggested by real life.

R. L. Stine

America is a great disappointment to me. As I said in one of my books, other societies create civilisations; we build shopping malls.

Bill Bryson

I have some shorter stories coming out in other books early next year. I might be pitching a re-vamp of Ghost Rider in the spring. We'll see.

Patton Oswalt

Comic books and graphic novels are a great medium. It's incredibly underused.

Darren Aronofsky

I think many of my books, including 'Handle with Care,' including 'My Sister's Keeper,' circle back to how far are we willing to go for the people we love? I think love changes the way we think. It's the thing that takes you out of what your normal set of beliefs would be.

Jodi Picoult

Books change us. Books save us. I know this because it happened to me. Books saved me. So, I do believe through stories we can learn to change, we can learn to empathize and be more connected with the universe and with humanity.

Elif Safak

Often the magical elements in my books are standing in for elements of the real world, the small and magical-in-their-own-right sorts of things that we take for granted and no longer pay attention to, like the bonds of friendship that entwine our own lives with those of other people and places.

Charles de Lint

I have to live my books before I write them.

Dave Ramsey

When I was working upon the ABC books, I wanted to show different ways that mainstream comics could viably have gone, that they didn't have to follow 'Watchmen' and the other 1980s books down this relentlessly dark route. It was never my intention to start a trend for darkness. I'm not a particularly dark individual.

Alan Moore

I'm not really one for reading books. I have a very poor attention span. I'd rather listen to music, play games or watch films on my iPad.

Olly Murs

I want to write such things as compel the admiring acclamation of the world at large, such things as are written but once in years, things subtle but distinctly different from the books written every day.

Mary MacLane

Jews have a special relationship to books, and the Haggadah has been translated more widely, and reprinted more often, than any other Jewish book. It is not a work of history or philosophy, not a prayer book, user's manual,

timeline, poem or palimpsest - and yet it is all these things.

Jonathan Safran Foer

Lovers of audio books learn to live with compromise.

David Sedaris

I'm a collecting maniac and I buy a lot of books and records. I have over thousand cds.

Ville Valo

For years I wrote in my basement. More recently I graduated to one floor above, an office with all my books and music and - ta da! - a window.

Mitch Albom

Conservatives should insist that defense spending be examined with the same seriousness that we demand in examining the books of those government agencies that spend taxpayer money in the name of welfare, the environment, or education.

Grover Norquist

My hardcover sales are 17% down in books but up 400% in electronics.

Lisa See

Oh, I was super serious about practicing and rudiments, and still am. I still have all my books.

Travis Barker

I have this fantasy. I'm walking past a bookshop and I click my fingers and all my books go blank. So I can start again and get it right.

John Banville

My first two books are out of print and, okay, they can sleep there comfortably. It's early work, derivative work.

Mary Oliver

The Cemetery of Forgotten Books is like the greatest, most fantastic library you could ever imagine. It's a labyrinth of books with tunnels, bridges, arches, secret sections - and it's hidden inside an old palace in the old city of Barcelona.

Carlos Ruiz Zafon

We should be as careful of the books we read, as of the company we keep. The dead very often have more power than the living.

Tryon Edwards

Books that change you, even later in life, give you a kind of electrical shock as the world takes a different shape.

A. S. Byatt

I'm not intelligent. I'm not arrogant. I'm just like the people who read my books. I used to have a jazz club, and I made the cocktails and I made the sandwiches. I didn't want to become a writer - it just happened.

Haruki Murakami

Most of us cluster somewhere in the middle of most statistical distributions. But there are lots of bell curves, and pretty much everyone is on a tail of at least one of them. We may collect strange memorabilia or read esoteric books, hold unusual religious beliefs or wear odd-sized shoes, suffer rare diseases or enjoy obscure movies.

Virginia Postrel

Books that distribute things... with as daring a freedom as we use in dreams, put us on our feet again.

Marsilio Ficino

I read the 'Twilight' books before the movie and the whole craze happened. And then I loved it. I was in love with Edward before every other girl that says she's in love with him was. Because I read them a long time ago shooting a movie in Salt Lake City, and one of Stephenie Meyer's friends said, 'Make sure you read my friend's book.'

Nina Dobrev

I'm not funny. People assume that because my books are funny, I'll be funny in real life. It's the inevitable disappointment of meeting me.

Jonathan Safran Foer

Every ceremony or rite has a value if it is performed without alteration. A ceremony is a book in which a great deal is written. Anyone who understands can read it. One rite often contains more than a hundred books.

George Gurdjieff

I review books as a day job, and through the years I've come to view the contemporary memoir as, almost always, a saga of victimization, sometimes by others, sometimes by the self, and sometimes by illness or misfortune, leading, like clockwork, to healing and redemption.

Walter Kirn

The coolest thing about the series is that we stay very true to the books; it would be silly for us not to, because the books are exactly what the fans want to see. There's an action side to it, which I love, and there are werewolves now. There aren't just vampires. There's a wolf pack.

Taylor Lautner

These are not books, lumps of lifeless paper, but minds alive on the shelves.

Gilbert Highet

The best books come from someplace inside. You don't write because you want to, but because you have to.

Judy Blume

Books, I found, had the power to make time stand still, retreat or fly into the future.

Jim Bishop

Oddly, the meanings of books are defined for me much more by their beginnings and middles than they are by their endings.

Lev Grossman

I'm reading a lot of different books, but I always think I have to switch it up a little bit. It's like food - everything in moderation, same with my books, same with my reading. You read books that are good for you and you learn a lot of stuff, then you read 'Fifty Shades of Grey,' which is like candy.

Shay Mitchell

I stole comic books from my brother when I was a kid, but I was never like an avid fan. I can't claim to be like a comic book geek.

Anna Kendrick

Movies are not scripts - movies are films; they're not books, they're not the theatre.

Nicolas Roeg

Cambridge was a joy. Tediously. People reading books in a posh place. It was my fantasy. I loved it. I miss it still.

Zadie Smith

After so many books and so many years of writing, I have a good idea of my strengths and weaknesses. I love the process of writing and, if I allowed myself, I would write far too much every day. One weakness which I've struggled to overcome is my tendency to having my characters ruminate for pages.

Walter Dean Myers

I used to get a haircut every Saturday so I would never miss any of the comic books. I had practically no hair when I was a kid!

R. L. Stine

As a child, I wanted only two things - to be left alone to read my library books, and to get away from my provincial hometown and go to London to be a writer. And I always knew that when I got there, I wanted to make loads of money.

Julie Burchill

My books are love stories at core, really. But I am interested in manifestations of love beyond the traditional romantic notion. In fact, I seem not particularly inclined to write romantic love as a narrative motive or as an easy source of happiness for my characters.

Khaled Hosseini

My favorite books are a constantly changing list, but one favorite has remained constant: the dictionary. Is the word I want to use spelled practice or practise? The dictionary knows. The dictionary also slows down my writing because it is such interesting reading that I am distracted.

Beverly Cleary

Because we do not sell photographs, we have no royalties on books, posters, postcards.

Christo

I had this desire to see the world. I couldn't see any of it, but I saw it in my imagination, and that's why I always read books, and I could go to Mars or Middle Earth or the Hyborian age.

George R. R. Martin

Nothing bores me more than books where you read two pages and you know exactly how it's going to come out. I want twists and turns that surprise me, characters that have a difficult time and that I don't know if they're going to live or die.

George R. R. Martin

The tendency of modern scientific teaching is to neglect the great books, to lay far too much stress upon relatively unimportant modern work, and to present masses of detail of doubtful truth and questionable weight in such a way as to obscure principles.

Ronald Fisher

I don't think we should see the world of books as

fundamentally separate from the world of the Internet. Yes, the Internet contains a lot of videos of squirrels riding skateboards, but it can also be a place that facilitates big conversations about books.

John Green

In quoting of books, quote such authors as are usually read; others you may read for your own satisfaction, but not name them.

John Selden

With twins, reading aloud to them was the only chance I could get to sit down. I read them picture books until they were reading on their own.

Beverly Cleary

The pleasure of all reading is doubled when one lives with another who shares the same books.

Katherine Mansfield

By the usual reckoning, the worst books make the best films.

Iain Banks

I'm a big illustration and comic book fan. In my eyes, comic books and illustration are the same kind of art forms.

Mika

I really enjoy making sure the kids get a healthy dinner, a good bath and several books... I really like to try and end the day with some quality time with my kids. If not, I feel guilty.

Norah O'Donnell

My first two books, 'Letters to a Young Brother' and 'Letters to a Young Sister,' were... distributed pretty widely. Judges in juvenile justice facilities started citing the book as required reading.

Hill Harper

Books about spies and traitors - and the congressional hearings that follow the exposure of traitors - generally assume that false-negative errors are much worse than false-positive errors.

Malcolm Gladwell

The fear of failure is so great, it is no wonder that the desire to do right by one's children has led to a whole library of books offering advice on how to raise them.

Bruno Bettelheim

I have to have a character worth caring about. I tend not to start writing books about people I don't have a lot of sympathy for because I'm just going to be with them too long.

Richard Russo

The stereotype of psychotherapy portrayed in popular books and movies is lying on the couch and saying whatever comes into your mind, while a kindly psychoanalyst listens and nods knowingly from time to time. After years and years, something wonderful is supposed to happen.

David D. Burns

I honestly don't read that much. Obviously I read chess books - in terms of favorites, Kasparov's 'My Great

Predecessors' is pretty good.

Magnus Carlsen

I like to make things, but I looked at old craft books on weaving or mosaics or whatever, I'm like, 'I don't really know anything about that stuff.'

Amy Sedaris

I did an audiobook for 'Rough Crossings,' which I thought was one of the best books I had published. But it was an absolute embarrassment to read it. All these horrible mucked-up bits of syntax, over-the-top adjectives. I found myself editing it while reading. Alert listeners will notice the difference.

Simon Schama

Learning is acquired by reading books, but the much more necessary learning, the knowledge of the world, is only to be acquired by reading men, and studying all the various facets of them.

Philip Stanhope, 4th Earl of Chesterfield

I'm a huge fan of Tolkien. I read those books when I was in junior high school and high school, and they had a profound effect on me. I'd read other fantasy before, but none of them that I loved like Tolkien.

George R. R. Martin

I love books and going to bookstores. My favorite sound is the sound of the needle hitting the record.

Winona Ryder

I know that the last thing a book wants is to just sit around unread, serving as an element of interior decorating. So when I have people over, all they have to do is glance at my books, and I implore them to take a few home with them. If I am really ambitious, I pack books into boxes and donate them to prisons.

Barbara Ehrenreich

All coffee shops now have WiFi. Why bring a book when you could be wittily attacking some idiot columnist on Twitter, or responding to your date requests, or posting a picture of your foot? All of that is more gripping and immediate and social than books.

Russell Smith

For a long time all I wanted for Christmas were books about outdoor survival. I was convinced that the woods were calling me. I camped a lot, I took classes. At 18, I told myself if I don't live in the woods by myself by the time I'm 25, I have failed.

Chris Evans

Nothing teaches great writing like the very best books do. Yet, good teachers often help students cross that bridge, and I have to say that I had a few extraordinary English teachers in high school whom I still credit for their guidance.

Julia Glass

Most of my life wasn't about knowledge from books, but experiential knowledge.

Matisyahu

If I'm home with no chore at hand, and a package of books has come, the television set and the chess board and the unanswered mail will have to manage without me if one of the books is a detective story.

Rex Stout

For myself, I haven't been content to carry on producing books that merely strain against the conventions - as I've grown older, and realised that there aren't that many books left for me to write, so I've become determined that they should be the fictive equivalent of ripping the damn corset off altogether and chucking it on the fire.

Will Self

I read my books aloud before they were published.

Beverly Cleary

Books are acts of composition: you compose them. You make music: the music is called fiction.

E. L. Doctorow

Even as the Internet has revived hope of a universal library and Google seems to promise an answer to every query, books have remained a dark region in the universe of information. We want books to be as accessible and searchable as the Web. On the other hand, we still want them to be books.

Gary Wolf

There are reasons people seek escape in books, and one of those reasons is that the boundary of what can happen is beyond what we do - or would want to see in real life.

James Patterson

You know, I have a lot of books on my iPad, but when I try to read them, I find myself wandering off to play games. Those are books I'm interested in. I can't imagine what would have happened to me in college if my biology class had been on the same computer as 'Words With Friends' and 'Doom.'

Gail Collins

Writing is a intensely personal activity. I can pen down my best thoughts when I'm alone. But when one is elevated into the stature of an author, you have to think about your books in terms of their business angle.

Ashwin Sanghi

In my next life, I want to be tall and thin, parallel park and make good coffee. But for now, I have lots of stuff to work

out in my life, but I'll have that until the day I die. I want to write more books.

Paula Danziger

Above all, the translation of books into digital formats means the destruction of boundaries. Bound, printed texts are discrete objects: immutable, individual, lendable, cut off from the world.

Tom Chatfield

When I climb into my car, I enter my destination into a GPS device, whose spatial memory supplants my own. I have photographs to store the images I want to remember, books to store knowledge and now, thanks to Google, I rarely have to remember anything more than the right set of search terms to access humankind's collective memory.

Joshua Foer

The fans that I have met so far have been nothing but supportive and extremely passionate about the books. I feel so honored to meet all these people. Something like this, which I think is bigger than anyone in the film, it's pretty crazy.

Liam Hemsworth

All those authors there, most of whom of course I've never met. That's the poetry side, that's the prose side, that's the fishing and miscellaneous behind me. You get an affection for books that you've enjoyed.

Norman MacCaig

Ramona was originally an accidental character I added to the Henry Huggins books because I noticed that none of the characters had siblings. I added Ramona as Beazus' pestering little sister.

Beverly Cleary

I wasn't smart enough to read relationship books when I was coming up. I learned everything the hard way.

Michael Ealy

If you're going to write about war, which my books are about, wars are nasty things. I think it's sort of a cheap, easy way out to write a war story in which no one ultimately dies.

George R. R. Martin

Americans think African writers will write about the exotic, about wildlife, poverty, maybe AIDS. They come to Africa and African books with certain expectations.

Chimamanda Ngozi Adichie

I have a real soft spot in my heart for librarians and people who care about books.

Ann Richards

I was obsessed with girls when I was 13 years old; I wasn't really into books.

Jamie Campbell Bower

I'm very comfortable with myself and my sexuality, but it doesn't define me. I also read books believe it or not.

Eva Mendes

After working with many nutritionists, reading books, and practicing trial and error on my own body, I have finally found a way to control my weight without deprivation. I call my program 'Somersizing,' and Somersizing is not a

diet. Diet is a nasty four-letter word that conjures up negative thoughts of sacrifice and obsession and guilt.

Suzanne Somers

How often have I met and disliked writers whose books I love; and conversely, hated the books and then wound up liking the writer? Too often.

Lev Grossman

Pat Moynihan could write books with one hand and legislate with the other. I can't; I have a short attention span. The slightest distraction would take me away from writing.

Barney Frank

The American people are screaming out saying it's unfair that the wealthiest, the largest corporations who can afford the best attorneys, the best accountants, take advantage of these special tax treatments that the lobbyists have, along with lawmakers, have cooked in the books here.

David Plouffe

In books, as in life, there are no second chances. On second thought: it's the next work, still to be written, that offers the second chance.

Cynthia Ozick

Feminism rotates between backlash and interest. And the cool thing about the Internet is that it's allowing women more access to their own history. Part of the problem before the Internet was that we didn't know which books to read. Someone had to tell you.

Kathleen Hanna

I still get up every morning at 4 A.M. I write seven days a week, including Christmas. And I still face a blank page every morning, and my characters don't really care how many books I've sold.

Dan Brown

I've always felt, in all my books, that there's a deep decency in the American people and a native intelligence - providing they have the facts, providing they have the information.

Studs Terkel

What irritates me is the bland way people go around saying, 'Oh, our attitude has changed. We don't dislike these people any more.' But by the strangest coincidence, they haven't taken away the injustice; the laws are still on the books.

Christopher Isherwood

Always in all my books I'm trying to reveal or help to reveal the hidden greatness of the small, of the little, of the unknown - and the pettiness of the big.

Eduardo Galeano

I have that love for music, when you are finding either old gems that you never heard or newer stuff that perks your ear. It keeps you trying to look for new stuff to write about it. You don't spin your wheels. I take that same approach to music and books.

Corey Taylor

I was a Marvel kid, and I would have to say that Spiderman is my all-time favorite character. As I got older, my tastes developed a little bit more, and I would follow certain writers; like, I really got into Grant Morrison. From the

time I was 5, I was into comic books. From the time I learned how to read, it was all about comic books.

Corey Taylor

With my adult books, for the first six weeks or so, it's about 60 percent ebooks in terms of sales. The kids' books, it's like 5 percent. Which means that the parents, the ones that aren't going into stores now, they're no longer buying books for their kids, which is not great.

James Patterson

Superman has evolved continually in the comic books over the course of 75 years. He couldn't even fly for years in the original comic books. Kryptonite wasn't added until the '60s. All sorts of things like this. If a character is going to remain vital, he does have to change with the times.

David S. Goyer

If an army of monkeys were strumming on typewriters, they might write all the books in the British Museum.

Arthur Eddington

Well, before I knew there was going to be a film. I was the biggest Harry Potter fan. I read all the books.

Rupert Grint

No matter how much time you spend reading books or following your intuition, you're gonna screw it up. Fifty times. You can't do parenting right.

Alan Arkin

I feel like the books were just written like a movie. You read it and you can just kind of see everything. Before I went in to read with the director, I read the first book and I loved it. I didn't realize how good the writing was. And then I went in and read with Gary Ross, and that was it.

Liam Hemsworth

I haven't been very enthusiastic about the commercialization of children's literature. Kids should borrow books from the library and not necessarily be buying them.

Beverly Cleary

Both my mum and dad were great readers, and we would go every Saturday morning to the library, and my sister and I had a library card when we could pass off something as a signature, and all of us would come with an armful of books.

Geraldine Brooks

Television isn't inherently good or bad. You go to a bookstore, there are how many thousands of books, but how many of those do you want? Five? Television's the same way. If you're going to show people stuff, television is the way to go. Words and pictures show things.

Bill Nye

Every day, I read books on philosophy and science fiction and human consciousness.

Tom DeLonge

I used to feel defensive when people would say, 'Yes, but your books have happy endings', as if that made them worthless, or unrealistic. Some people do get happy endings, even if it's only for a while. I would rather never be published again than write a downbeat ending.

Marian Keyes

People who don't normally read make an exception for my books, possibly because they're short.

Mitch Albom

I'm aware of 'Twilight,' but I've never seen the movies or read any of the books. Frankly, the story leaves me cold - why do a vampire story about abstinence?

Alan Ball

Doctoral training is devoted almost entirely to learning to do research, even though most Ph.Ds who enter academic life spend far more time teaching than they do conducting experiments or writing books.

Derek Bok

There is the myth that writing books for children is easier than writing books for grownups, whereas we know that truly great books for children are works of genius, whether it's 'Alice in Wonderland' or the 'Gruffalo' or 'Northern Lights.' When it's a great book, it's a great book, whether it's for children or not.

Michael Morpurgo

What I mean by that is that the point of life, as I see it, is not to write books or scale mountains or sail oceans, but to achieve happiness, and preferably an unselfish happiness.

Bernard Cornwell

As the 2012 elections approach the finish line, the chatter among columnists and political reporters is about upcoming books that take readers inside the campaigns, cutting-edge efforts to micro-target voters on Internet social applications, the enormous money flowing through super-PACs, and extreme political polarization.

Juan Williams

Sometimes I don't like the books that I'm reading.

Charlie Kaufman

My platform has been to reach reluctant readers. And one of the best ways I found to motivate them is to connect them with reading that interests them, to expand the definition of reading to include humor, science fiction/fantasy, nonfiction, graphic novels, wordless books, audio books and comic books.

Jon Scieszka

Books are in no hurry. An act of creation is in no hurry; it reads us, it privileges us infinitely. The notion that it is the occasion for our cleverness fills me with baffled bitterness and anger.

George Steiner

'The Hunger Games' for me is I love the books so much and the character and the story were incredible. That's kind of the game plan is just do really interesting stories with interesting characters.

Josh Hutcherson

A bibliophile of little means is likely to suffer often. Books don't slip from his hands but fly past him through the air, high as birds, high as prices.

William Lyon Phelps

People, and especially theologians, should try to familiarize themselves with scientific ideas. Of course, science is technical in many respects, but there are some very good books that try to set out some of the conceptual structure of

science.

John Polkinghorne

I have to have three or four books going simultaneously. If I'm not impressed in the first 20 pages, I don't bother reading the rest, especially with novels. I'm not a book-club style reader. I'm not looking for life lessons or wanting people to think I'm smart because I'm reading a certain book.

Chris Abani

Every year the literary press praises dozens if not hundreds of novels to the skies, asserting explicitly or implicitly that these books will probably not be suffering water damage in the basements of their authors' houses 20 years from now. But historically, anyway, that's not the way the novelistic ecology works.

Lev Grossman

Travel books are, by and large, boring. They lodge uncomfortably between fact, fiction and autobiography.

Arthur Smith

What's interesting about books that take place in the future, even twenty years in the future, is that many of them are black or white: It's either a utopia or it's misery. The real truth is that there's going to be both things in any future, just like there is now.

Albert Brooks

My son was born during my last semester in college. His due date was Thanksgiving, but he didn't show up until finals week. I brought my books to the hospital and didn't think anything of it. That is what a father is supposed to do.

LZ Granderson

The shelves of many evangelicals are full of books that point out the flaws in evolution, discuss it only as a theory, and almost imply that there's a conspiracy here to avoid the fact that evolution is actually flawed. All of those books, unfortunately, are based upon conclusions that no reasonable biologist would now accept.

Francis Collins

Books aren't written - they're rewritten. Including your own. It is one of the hardest things to accept, especially after the seventh rewrite hasn't quite done it.

Michael Crichton

Like any small business owner, I experienced the pressures of building a company from the ground up - developing a business plan, balancing the books, meeting payroll and building a customer base.

Gavin Newsom

I've spent most of my life trying to wear a persona that didn't quite fit and when I started writing books, it was like finally becoming the right person.

Meg Rosoff

I grew up in a small town in India, but through books I knew the world.

Mira Nair

I teethed on books of heroes such as Winston Churchill, Abraham Lincoln and King David.

Luke Ford

Wherever you look there are inspirations, books, literature, paintings, landscapes, everything. Just living is an inspiration.

Gavin Rossdale

Fashion is a very stressful place to work because of the demands of doing the shows - no one expects a writer to produce two books a year on the dot - but it's also a very toxic place to work.

John Galliano

I was always a big fan of the books and over the years I've become quite attached to Ron and we've meshed into the same person, really.

Rupert Grint

I remember being shocked when I discovered some of my school pals didn't have books in their homes. I thought it was like not having oxygen, or hot water.

Iain Banks

Sometimes I can tackle an issue -homelessness, tobacco

litigation, insurance fraud, the death penalty - and wrap a good story around it. These are the best books, the ones with a story and a message.

John Grisham

'Harry Potter' opened so many doors for young adult literature. It really did convince the publishing industry that writing for children was a viable enterprise. And it also convinced a lot of people that kids will read if we give them books that they care about and love.

Rick Riordan

I think children love reading, and they will make time for it if we put the right books into their hands. And I hope I get the chance to keep being one of the people that writes them.

Rick Riordan

The deeper I go into mythology, the more I find. I originally did five 'Percy Jackson' books. I thought that would cover Greek mythology and I couldn't have been more wrong. It's ever-expanding.

Rick Riordan

My mother had all these maxims - like, classy girls never chew gum, never read comic books, never get their ears pierced, never get their hair dyed.

Jennifer Tilly

You're getting to know who the great chefs are through their books.

Thomas Keller

Most of the great books on prayer are written by 'experts' - monks, missionaries, mystics, saints. I've read scores of them, and mainly they make me feel guilty.

Philip Yancey

Stephen King in many respects is a wonderful writer. He has made a contribution. People in the future will be able to pick up Stephen King's books and learn a lot about who we were by reading those books.

Anne Rice

Digital television, satellite radio, videogames, iPods - so much media. Do books even matter anymore?

Mo Rocca

The science can tell you that the thousands of pseudo-scientific parenting books out there - not to mention the 'Baby Einstein' DVDs and the flash cards and the brain-boosting toys - won't do a thing to make your baby smarter. That's largely because babies are already as smart as they can be; smarter than we are in some ways.

Alison Gopnik

With so many forty- and fifty something mums and dads in Converse stalking the streets, I can see why there's a slew of books about the menopause and middle age, the most recent addition being David Bainbridge's plucky, glass-half-full meditation or, as he calls it, 'natural history.'

Rachel Johnson

I don't often reread my own books, unless I am going into another in the series and need to refresh my mood when originating the concept.

Anne McCaffrey

I'm no different from anybody else. If I don't have a card, I

can't check out these books.

Bess Truman

Printed books usually outlive bookstores and the publishers who brought them out. They sit around, demanding nothing, for decades. That's one of their nicest qualities - their brute persistence.

Nicholson Baker

Whether it's viewers of the show or readers of my columns and books, I'm consistently impressed with their wit, humor and insight. That goes for about 95 percent of the audience. The other five percent are why the 'Delete' option and restraining orders were invented.

Richard Roeper

I'm not one of those professors whose office is encased floor-to-ceiling with books. By the way, I think academics do this to intimidate their visitors.

Gary Hamel

I would never require anyone to read any book. That seems

antithetical to why we read - which is to choose a book for our personal reasons. I always shudder when I'm told my books are on required reading lists.

Amy Tan

Slightly embarrassing admission: Even when I was a kid, I used to have these little spy books, and I would, like, see what everybody was doing in my neighborhood and log it down.

Heather Brooke

When I was eight years old, I got a dummy for Christmas and started teaching myself. I got books and records and sat in front of the bathroom mirror, practising. I did my first show in the third grade and just kept going; there was no reason to quit.

Jeff Dunham

A border collie named Orson inspired me to buy a 110-acre farm with four barns and a sheep. That led to a series of books about Bedlam Farm and about dogs, rural life, lambing and herding sheep.

Jon Katz

The U.S. has a law on the books called the debt limit, but the name is misleading. The debt limit started in 1917 for the purpose of facilitating more national debt, not reducing it. It still serves that purpose. It's unconnected to spending, hurts our credit rating and has been an abject failure at limiting debt.

David Malpass

I only work on my books at nights and at weekends. It is really just like a hobby.

Jeff Kinney

Finishing books - and leaving the world you've created - is always a kind of emotionally wrenching experience. I usually cry.

Lauren Oliver

The fate of the singers who, like my songs, went up in flame was also the fate of the books which I later wrote. All of them went up in flame to Heaven in a fire which broke out one night at my home in Bad Homburg as I lay ill in a hospital.

Shmuel Yosef Agnon

Books won't stay banned. They won't burn. Ideas won't go to jail.

Alfred Whitney Griswold

The great thing about books is that you can end with a question mark.

Joanne Harris

I just love comic books. I've always loved comic book art, and I just think it's amazing.

Zayn Malik

Standing as a witness in all things means all things - big things, little things, in all conversations, in jokes, in games played and books read and music listened to, in causes supported, in service rendered, in clothes worn, in friends made.

Margaret D. Nadauld

We didn't have a whole lot of money when I was growing up either. I would always ask for magic books or magic tricks for my birthday or for Christmas and the rest of the year I either had to mow lawns or find part time jobs to help supplement the cost of doing magic.

Lance Burton

I didn't really like reading much before I did 'The Golden Compass'. But then my teacher told me to read it. And I thought, 'Oh God, I'm going to have to read a whole book by myself!' It's not that I couldn't read, it's just that I didn't really like books very much. But the book that she lent me I really enjoyed.

Dakota Blue Richards

I'm not itching to sue Amazon or Wal-Mart... they sell a lot of books. But the future is very uncertain with books.

John Grisham

I have a very low tolerance for boredom and often think I would have missed out on books entirely if I'd grown up in the Internet and video game age. Now I enjoy books for people of all ages, including children.

Rick Yancey

I love real books, paper books, but I also love buying online, and I think that people are more willing to take a chance to read something if it's cheaper - sometimes books on the Kindle are $6. A hardback book is $25. For $25, it better be a really great book. Or you're going to be mad.

Caroline Leavitt

Word books traditionally focus on unusual and quirky items. They tend to ignore the words that provide the skeleton of the language, without which it would fall apart, such as 'and' and 'what,' or words that provide structure to our conversation, such as 'hello.'

David Crystal

I need a stimulating environment to write because my books are driven at 100 miles per hour at a time.

Lee Child

Travel teaches as much as books.

Youssou N'Dour

I have an obsession with books about kids with Asperger's syndrome.

Donald Glover

I don't set out to transmit a message. I don't write with a political point of view. There are no religious overtones. Looking back at my books, I can say, 'Oh, yes, it is there.' But it's not in my mind when I write.

Lois Lowry

But, you know, I just did a big trip in the spring to Vietnam and Cambodia and Thailand, and that's when I bought a Kindle. I have like 15 books on this one little gizmo. But when I came home, the first night I picked up the book that was on my nightstand and I went right back to that.

Lisa See

I came to think that nobody from England could draw American comic books, because they were clearly all done by this sort of Mafia, all these guys with Italian and Irish names who had the whole thing sewn up. It was actually seeing a comic book drawn by Barry Smith, who was about my age, and English.

Dave Gibbons

Guys that preach verse-by-verse through books of the Bible - that is just cheating. It's cheating because that would be easy, first of all. That isn't how you grow people. No one in the Scripture modeled that.

Andy Stanley

A man loses contact with reality if he is not surrounded by his books.

Francois Mitterrand

Every well-written book is a light for me. When you write, you use other writers and their books as guides in the wilderness.

Kate DiCamillo

When I was growing up, my house was filled with books. My mother was an educator, and my father was a history buff, so our home was a virtual library, covering every author from Beverly Cleary to James Michener.

Jeff Kinney

As a result of playing Freddy Krueger, I can remember having to look at some medical books, and at some of the disfigurement that fire can cause on people, because they were the source material for some of the prosthetic makeup that I wore. That aided and abetted this fear of death by fire. Which is sort of what happened to Fred Krueger.

Robert Englund

I loved doing problems in school. I'd take them home and make up new ones of my own. But the best problem I ever found, I found in my local public library. I was just browsing through the section of math books and I found this one book, which was all about one particular problem - Fermat's Last Theorem.

Andrew Wiles

My childhood was surrounded by books and writing. From a very early age I was fascinated by storytelling, by the printed word, by language, by ideas. So I would seek them out.

Carlos Ruiz Zafon

I think people ease into this careerist professionalism, so if you're a writer it's your job to manufacture books as opposed to writing them and to go to festivals and spend

your life emotionally invested in reviews or the awards. You have to shrink your universe in a way. To me, it's the opposite.

Arundhati Roy

You will find something more in woods than in books. Trees and stones will teach you that which you can never learn from masters.

Saint Bernard

I cannot live without books.

Thomas Jefferson

The book salesman should be honored because he brings to our attention, as a rule, the very books we need most and neglect most.

Confucius

Those who decide to use leisure as a means of mental development, who love good music, good books, good pictures, good plays, good company, good conversation - what are they? They are the happiest people in the world.

William Lyon Phelps

I've gotten books published. I've met famous people that are very nice. I look back and I say, 'Wow. Thank you, God, for giving me this gift. And thank you for helping me to keep going.'

Mattie Stepanek

Expand the definition of 'reading' to include non-fiction, humor, graphic novels, magazines, action adventure, and, yes, even websites. It's the pleasure of reading that counts; the focus will naturally broaden. A boy won't read shark books forever.

Jon Scieszka

All the ills of mankind, all the tragic misfortunes that fill the history books, all the political blunders, all the failures of the great leaders have arisen merely from a lack of skill at dancing.

Moliere

I remember when I was very young, I had a fever - a long rheumatic fever in bed for four months. And in the days, I

stayed alone with the maid. I only had my father's books with me. They were fantasy books about ghosts, and also books by Edgar Allen Poe that made a forever impression on me.

Dario Argento

I don't read books by people who have betrayed the Motherland.

Vladimir Putin

Wisdom is not wisdom when it is derived from books alone.

Horace

To study the phenomena of disease without books is to sail an uncharted sea, while to study books without patients is not to go to sea at all.

William Osler

What a circus act we women perform every day of our lives. Look at us. We run a tightrope daily, balancing a pile of books on the head. Baby-carriage, parasol, kitchen chair,

still under control. Steady now! This is not the life of simplicity but the life of multiplicity that the wise men warn us of.

Anne Morrow Lindbergh

Real education should consist of drawing the goodness and the best out of our own students. What better books can there be than the book of humanity?

Cesar Chavez

A single conversation across the table with a wise man is better than ten years mere study of books.

Henry Wadsworth Longfellow

There were times, especially when I was traveling for 'Eat, Pray, Love,' when, I swear to God, I would feel this weight of my female ancestors, all those Swedish farmwives from beyond the grave who were like, 'Go! Go to Naples! Eat more pizza! Go to India, ride an elephant! Do it! Swim in the Indian Ocean. Read those books. Learn a language.'

Elizabeth Gilbert

My Alma mater was books, a good library... I could spend the rest of my life reading, just satisfying my curiosity.

Malcolm X

Titles are important; I have them before I have books that belong to them. I have last chapters in my mind before I see first chapters, too. I usually begin with endings, with a sense of aftermath, of dust settling, of epilogue.

John Irving

The books that will never be read. And all due to the fear of censorship. As always, young readers will be the real losers.

Judy Blume

The Bible is one of the most genocidal books in history.

Noam Chomsky

In the dime stores and bus stations, people talk of situations, read books, repeat quotations, draw conclusions on the wall.

Bob Dylan

It's in the history books, the Holocaust. It's just a phrase. And the truth is it happened yesterday. It happened to my mother. I never met my grandmothers or my grandfathers. They were all wiped up in the gas chambers of Nazi Germany.

Gene Simmons

Books are the carriers of civilization. Without books, history is silent, literature dumb, science crippled, thought and speculation at a standstill.

Barbara Tuchman

My mum was never too keen on TV, so we kids all went to the library and got books out. Right from the start, I loved the works of Mark Twain. Every time I read about Tom Sawyer, I'd go out and do something low-level naughty, just like him.

John Grisham

We used to root for the Indians against the cavalry, because we didn't think it was fair in the history books that when the cavalry won it was a great victory, and when the Indians won it was a massacre.

Dick Gregory

I have always loved and avidly read the novels of Jack London, Jules Verne and Ernest Hemingway. The characters depicted in their books, who are brave and resourceful people embarking on exciting adventures, definitely shaped my inner self and nourished my love for the outdoors.

Vladimir Putin

I am a big defender of 'Harry Potter,' and I think any book that gets kids to read are books that we should cherish, we should be thankful for them.

Judy Blume

It's funny that I got to do 'On the Road' because the thing that had the biggest impact on me growing up was reading books. I was very inspired by the book and this spirit of Dean Moriarty and how envious we all are of somebody who can be that carefree.

Garrett Hedlund

Whether I'm being influenced by new music that I'm

listening to, books I've read, my friends, or my faith, I'm learning all the time.

Hayley Williams

I definitely subscribe to the idea that 9/11, to use an overused phrase, was a wake-up call. There was a year-long national teach-in on Islam - everyone read books and suddenly talked about Islam, and that was very productive. But there's no doubt that moment has passed.

Bruce Feiler

Do not suppose, however, that I intend to urge a diet of classics on anybody. I have seen such diets at work. I have known people who have actually read all, or almost all, the guaranteed Hundred Best Books. God save us from reading nothing but the best.

Robertson Davies

I believe in originality, primarily. However, it's important to know what there has been before to aim in that direction. Art history informs us. It informs our mind. I like to look at books, exhibitions, paintings, as a computer, subconsciously taking on information.

Philip Treacy

Why do I write books? Why do I think? Why should I be passionate? Because things could be different, they could be made better.

Zygmunt Bauman

Two things I do well in books are sex and violence, but I don't want gratuitous sex or violence. The sex and violence are only as graphic as need be. And never included unless it furthers the plot or character development.

Laurell K. Hamilton

I'm a big online everything. But for me, shopping online started with music, obviously, then it went onto books, meditation CDs, and I just recently bought these electronic cigarettes. My husband is trying to quit smoking, so I went online and I bought those BluCigs cigarettes in every flavor for him.

Fergie

I had already done a lot of research for Rough Riders, keeping notebooks and old photographs. Some of the books were antiques for that time period, with the covers falling off.

Tom Berenger

When I write, I try to think back to what I was afraid of or what was scary to me, and try to put those feelings into books.

R. L. Stine

Books on horse racing subjects have never done well, and I am told that publishers had come to think of them as the literary version of box office poison.

Laura Hillenbrand

I think people in Botswana are pleased that my books paint a positive picture of their lives and portray the country as being very special. They've made a great success of their country, and the people are fed up with the constant reporting of only the problems and poverty of the continent. They welcome something which puts the positive side.

Alexander McCall Smith

I will write a couple of books and become a millionaire.

Stieg Larsson

I read true crime books, and I read when people do case studies of stuff. I'm into books like that. Case studies or forensics or murder - all that good stuff.

Tom Araya

I started by just sitting by the chessboard exploring things. I didn't even have books at first, and I just played by myself. I learnt a lot from that, and I feel that it is a big reason why I now have a good intuitive understanding of chess.

Magnus Carlsen

I don't really have a domestic inclination. Even my apartment has a semblance of a storage facility. It's just stacks, there are no bookshelves, just books and piles of stamp collections and weird little sewing and knitting projects.

Sufjan Stevens

It's just different discipline, just doing the voice over. I guess I've done about 5 or 6 audio books in the past and I do the animated voice for a show called Fatherhood on Nickelodeon.

Blair Underwood

We had many books and pictures... my parents' way of life doubtless left a lasting impression on me. They created an atmosphere in which a certain kind of freedom could exist. This may well account for my seeking a related sense of liberty as I grew up.

Alfred Stieglitz

My life's goal is not to write books; my life's goal is to know God better today. The neat thing about a goal like that is you can achieve it. Faith is constant; it's a relationship.

Anne Graham Lotz

The memoir industry is, what's the word? Under regulated. I think it needs to be pruned. If there are too many books right now and the market for readers is shrinking, I think we can get rid of many of the memoirs. Another memoir should be awfully well justified before it gets published.

Arthur Phillips

I am a crazy online shopper. My husband always jokes,

'Another box arrived!' Airplanes used to be my sanctuary for reading books, but now I have to peruse Gilt sales.

Lisa Ling

When I go on vacation, I take very few clothes and a whole lot of books. It's the most soothing thing in the world. Reading 'Moby-Dick' is like being in a time machine. I almost feel as excited as the first time I read it and I always find something new.

Nile Rodgers

I remember that I used to get lots of books from the library, and 'Little Women' was one of them. And I used to just cross out the parts of it that really upset me because it's such a sad book in so many ways. I'd cross out the parts that upset me, and I would rewrite new endings.

Helen Oyeyemi

Accolades and lists may tell us about accomplishments, but life is meant to be experienced, not just accomplished. It's like the difference between reading books for the sake of reading and reading books just to get a good grade.

LZ Granderson

Kids are so fiercely opinionated, that if they love the Harry Potter books and they go see the movie, they'll be the first to say, 'That was wrong! They didn't get that right!' They're storytellers themselves. They're critics. They're going to have the critical opinion.

Spike Jonze

Looking back, I realize my favorite stories weren't in books, they were in comics. On top of being a history enthusiast, my father was also a comics fan, and he kept his stash in the top drawer of his dresser, in easy reach of a kid making a beeline to the bathroom.

Jeff Kinney

A reactionary is someone who wants to return to a previous state - that's never a possibility in my books. For me, everything's irreversible in the life of a society, as well as an individual's.

Michel Houellebecq

I grew up reading comic books, pulp books, mystery and science fiction and fantasy. I'm a geek; I make no pretensions otherwise. It's the stuff that I love writing

about. I like creating worlds.

David S. Goyer

My first book was the most successful debut novel in the U.K. ever and every one of my books has reached number one in the U.K. Clearly the British know brilliance when they see it.

Kathy Reichs

There is no question that creative intelligence comes not through learning things you find in books or histories that have already been written, but by focusing on and giving value to experience as it happens.

Antony Gormley

I thought about cricket a lot. I needed to get out of this bubble of mine. I found it in books and conversations with other people about other things. I was a curious person, and this was my release. I like being challenged intellectually. I hated at the end of the day to talk cricket to someone else.

Rahul Dravid

Music is gathering. Taking our scattered thoughts and senses and coalescing us back into our core. Music is powerful. The first few chords can change us where no self-help books can.

Jane Siberry

The deadlines are much, much longer with books. When I was a reporter, a lot of times I'd come in at 8:30 a.m., get an assignment right away, interview somebody, turn the story in by 9:30, and have the finished story in the paper that landed on my desk by noon.

Margaret Haddix

There are six 'Time Warp Trio' books that would take a page each to fully praise. And I just thought up twelve more while I was typing this sentence.

Jon Scieszka

Lists of books we reread and books we can't finish tell more about us than about the relative worth of the books themselves.

Russell Banks

I'm famously secretive about my work. Nobody reads my books till they're finished.

Sarah Dessen

The one thing that I would say that defines me is I love to learn. I get excited about new things. I buy more books than I read or finish.

Satya Nadella

There is a lot of talk in publishing these days that we need to become more like the Internet: We need to make books for short attention spans with bells and whistles - books, in short, that are as much like 'Angry Birds' as possible. But I think that's a terrible idea.

John Green

I went to work in an office and learned, among other lessons, to do things I did not care for, and to do them well. Before I left this office, two of my books had already been published.

Sigrid Undset

All of my books have the potential to become movies, it's just a question of finding a studio who wants to get behind me and put up the money to make the movie.

Jackie Collins

I know that I am very popular in Holland, in fact I have visited Amsterdam several times to publicize my books. I have a great publisher in Holland and they have published all of my books in Dutch.

Jackie Collins

I like the idea of making big budget films with a heart. I like graphic novels more than comic books.

Matthew Vaughn

I am not that attached to material things. And the good thing is I can make choices. I have very few possessions. Luckily, as a man you don't need much... a few papers, a couple of books, and a few shirts, jackets, sweaters. It fits in a little thing, in a paper bag, so it's very easy.

Nicolas Berggruen

Books give not wisdom where none was before. But where some is, there reading makes it more.

Elizabeth Hardwick

I do so much revising as I go along; I wonder how I could write books if I hadn't grown up in the computer age. I think I'd be a very different writer. I find myself cutting and pasting, changing things around and deleting whole paragraphs constantly.

Megan McCafferty

In a fit at the bookstore one day, I bought all my favourite composers' biographies: Schubert, Massenet, Wolf. I've still not had a chance to read them; it breaks my heart. But when you travel so much, you just can't take that many books with you.

Danielle de Niese

My mom didn't write, but she loved to read. She liked books 'that made you a little nervous.' Stephen King, Dean Koontz and Peter Straub were the three wise men of our family bookshelf.

Michael Easton

If you grow up in Ireland and read books then you really are obliged to attempt your own some time. It is not exactly a choice. I still don't know if I am a writer. Believe me, there are days when I have my doubts.

Anne Enright

I know that for every reader who has lost the habit or can't find the time, there are people who've never enjoyed reading and question the value of literature, either as entertainment or education, or believe that a love of books, and of fiction in particular, is sentimental or frivolous.

David Nicholls

Carnegie Hall is as good as they say it is. It's not like Stonehenge which looks great in books but then you go there and it's a pile of rocks next to a highway. There's actually a highway right next to it, but you don't see that in pictures.

Bill Burr

I don't plot the books out ahead of time, I don't plan them. I don't begin at the beginning and end at the end. I don't work with an outline and I don't work in a straight line.

Diana Gabaldon

Being a journalist is good if you want to write books: it teaches you to get beyond the blank screen. My books have been described as froth, but there's scope to be witty and ironic about everything in life.

Sophie Kinsella

Not as ours the books of old - Things that steam can stamp and fold; Not as ours the books of yore - Rows of type, and nothing more.

Henry Austin Dobson

My gut feeling is that paper and ink are going to be with us for a long time yet, and in substantial quantities, though certainly books are now going to be available in other forms.

Fred Saberhagen

I have always loved animals, and as a child, I read a lot of horse books. I had a particular favorite called 'Silver Snaffles' that my mother gave away.

Drew Gilpin Faust

Schools and libraries are the twin cornerstones of a civilized society. Libraries are only good if people use them, like books only exist when someone reads them.

Nicholas Meyer

The American mind, unlike the English, is not formed by books, but, as Carl Sandburg once said to me... by newspapers and the Bible.

Van Wyck Brooks

Listen, I wrote 10 unsuccessful books before I broke through, so I'm looking all the time to keep my books fascinating. I want to write what people want to read, not push any message.

Ken Follett

You don't hear TV cops griping because they have to enforce some Draconian law that shouldn't be on the books in the first place, or lamenting vindictive excesses in sentencing. Hollywood, supposedly a frothing cauldron of liberalism, has always been conservative on crime.

Tom Shales

Well Ice H20 is my company that I plan to take to the next level with new artists, books, movies and so forth. It's more like a multimedia brand that I want to take to the next level and put some talented people on.

Raekwon

Almost every morning I write in my journal. I've been keeping it for a long time - I've filled more than 50 books. I write about what's going on in my personal and spiritual life or what's going on at work. It helps me keep things in perspective, especially when things get crazy or I get stressed or we have obstacles.

Blake Mycoskie

I was big into mythology when I was a kid - Arthurian legends and Greek mythology, that was kind of my passion. I hadn't heard of the books, but I was told they were very popular amongst the kids, so I got a hold of them and read them. I totally got it!

Steve Valentine

I know that I'm already in the history books and that people are going to remember me as the prisoner of war and the fabricated stories, but you know, to me I was just another soldier over there doing my job.

Jessica Lynch

All of my books come from pain.

Bret Easton Ellis

But you can try to read books at the wrong time or for the wrong reasons.

Jonathan Coe

I'd always liked to read, but when I picked up books I wasn't getting the same kind of excitement from them that I was from going out clubbing. I wanted to get the same kind of feel.

Irvine Welsh

Study nature, not books.

Louis Agassiz

There's a famous tension between Green Lantern and Green Arrow in the comic books. Those guys have always been friends. They started off as not on the same page, and then they quickly became best friends.

Geoff Johns

Living wild species are like a library of books still unread. Our heedless destruction of them is akin to burning the library without ever having read its books.

John Dingell

My first job out of college was as an editorial assistant in a New York publishing house. Being an editorial assistant is the purgatory would-be editors must endure before they can ascend the ladder and begin acquiring books on their own. I spent a year filing paperwork, writing copy, and typing rejection letters.

Lincoln Child

I am really impressed by lawyers who write books and tell us that they never lost a case. Most lawyers who have never lost a case have not had enough hard cases. But there are very difficult cases out there.

Floyd Abrams

Teen problem novels? I can go through them like a box of chocolates. And there are fantasy books out now that need a lot more editing. Fantasy got to be so popular that people began to think 'We don't need to be as diligent with the razor blade,' but they do.

Tamora Pierce

Why do we have a brain in the first place? Not to write books, articles, or plays; not to do science or play music. Brains develop because they are an expedient way of managing life in a body.

Antonio Damasio

As a youngster, I used to try to pick up any bits of wisdom about the guitar I could. It's not like now where you have books and books about every aspect of anything. Any little pearl of wisdom was welcome back then.

Johnny Marr

I've read all the 'Game of Thrones' books many times over, so I sometimes find it easier being on set, because it can be

hard to get out of character.

Emilia Clarke

As a child I was really into fantasy books with elves and goblins and swords, and I went through a phase for a few years when I was reading endless series. But in the end I became totally fed-up with all these sub-Tolkien rip-offs because they all end up doing the same old things and there's no rigour to it.

Jonathan Stroud

Some say it is the elements of hope and wonder in children's books that make them special. But there are many dark young adult novels these days. Adults loved Harry Potter, though it was written for the young. In the end, it is probably up to the reader of any age to decide if this book is for him or her.

Katherine Paterson

My complaint is that there are more books and news articles than there are primary scientific papers. I am probably the biggest critic of the hypesters, because it's dangerous when fields get overhyped.

Craig Venter

If I loved all the world as I do you, I shouldn't write books to it: I should only write letters to it, and that would be only a clumsy stage on the way to entire telepathy.

Laurence Housman

'Oh, the Places You'll Go!,' by Dr. Seuss, is still one of my favorite books ever.

Hilary Swank

Romance novels are my favorite books to read. I write young adult romances, and am so happy to be promoting this wonderful genre.

Simone Elkeles

Teenage readers also have a different relationship with the authors whose work they value than adult readers do. I loved Toni Morrison, but I don't have any desire to follow her on Twitter. I just want to read her books.

John Green

I love old books. They tell you stories about their use. You

can see where the fingerprints touched the pages as they held the book open. You can see how long they lingered on each page by the finger stains.

Jack Bowman

I have written 20 books, and each one is like having a baby. Writing is not easy; some people want to write books but just can't put a story together. I can put together a story that interests both me and my readers.

Jackie Collins

If Google Books is successful, others will follow.

Sergey Brin

A harsh reality of newspaper editing is that the deadlines don't allow for the polish that you expect in books or even magazines.

Bill Walsh

I don't care how I got here. In the books, when you look at it 10 or 20 years from now, it's not going say how he got here, it's going to say he's here and he represented the team.

Vince Carter

I taught elementary school and painted apartments for ten years. Now I write full-time and never have to change a thing I write. Every book comes to me in a flash of inspiration and takes me about two seconds to finish. The longer books, like the 'Time Warp Trio' novels, take a little longer to write - more like four seconds.

Jon Scieszka

People say, 'All my son will read is 'Captain Underpants,' or 'My son is crazy about shark books, is that O.K.?' I want to be the person to say, 'Yeah, that's really O.K., as long as he's motivated to want to read.'

Jon Scieszka

I like writing for children. It seems to me that most people underestimate their understanding and the strength of their feelings and in my books for them I try to put this right.

Nina Bawden

I had amazing intellectual privilege as a kid. My mom taught me to read when I was two or three. When I was

five, I read and wrote well enough to do my nine-year older brother's homework in exchange for chocolate or cigarettes. By the time I was 10, I was reading Orwell, Tolstoy's 'War and Peace,' and the Koran. I was reading comic books, too.

Chris Abani

I do the same things I did when I was 12 years old: I ride bikes, I read books, I walk in the woods. And I listen to music.

Charles Frazier

One time at the University of Colorado, at a faculty dinner, this professor said to me, 'Well, my goodness, a boy from Appa-lay-chee-a with a Ph.D!' The dinner was in her house. And I said, 'My grandparents didn't have indoor plumbing, but they had more books in their house than you do.' I was a little insulted by the Appa-lay-chee-a business.

Charles Frazier

Putting lessons in young adult books is very dangerous.

Ned Vizzini

We never had books at home, but my dad, seeing how keen I was to read, took me to Islington Library when I was about eight and we pulled out two - a Biggles and a science fiction novel. I never got the ace fighter pilot but fell in love with all things to do with the future and space. Isaac Asimov soon became my guiding star.

Gary Kemp

Whether it is the cavemen in the caves thousands of years ago, Shakespeare plays, television, movies and books, stories and characters take us on a journey. All I do is tell those stories without scripts and without actors.

Mark Burnett

My interest in society - at times so pronounced that the word 'snob' comes a little to mind - derives from the fact that I like an immense number of things which society, money, and position bring in their train: painting, tapestries, rare books, smart dresses, dances, gardens, country houses, correct cuisine, and pretty women.

Frank Crowninshield

Some say I'm an overnight success. Well, that was a very long night that lasted about 10 years. But while I do, of course, now feel the pressure having had books that have

been very successful, I just know I have to concentrate on writing for myself. I can't worry about genres or markets or what might be commercial or not. That never works.

Kate Morton

Normally, I could hit hard enough, as anyone who studied my fights might have known. But the impression was that I was essentially defensive, the very reverse of a killer, the prize fighter who read books, even Shakespeare.

Gene Tunney

As I got older, I really got into Tupac's poetry, his books and just learning about his life and what he was into.

Jhene Aiko

I've had a lot of books rejected in my time. My first novel, which didn't get published, was, with hindsight, crashingly dull.

Helen Fielding

I bought some books in order to learn the first principles of philosophy.

Johann Heinrich Lambert

I think books that are meant to be read in the nighttime ought to confront the very fears that we're trying to think about.

Daniel Handler

What I find cool about being a banned author is this: I'm writing books that evoke a reaction, books that, if dropped in a lake, go down not with a whimper but a splash.

Lauren Myracle

I grew up around books. When I first held the book and it was a substantive, tangible thing, and I thought of all the work that went into it, not just my work but everybody else's and the research and so forth, there's a sense of really have done something worthwhile.

Paul Allen

I wanted the feel in these books to be like an epic fantasy, with kings, queens, dukes and court politics, but of course like what I was explaining before, about making the science make sense, you have to make the politics make sense, too.

Kevin J. Anderson

I feel like 'Gossip Girl' isn't really 'Gossip Girl' anymore when they're away at school because they don't go to NYU; they go to, like, Yale and Brown. New York City is just as much a character as anyone else in the books, and I was really sort of reluctant to show them off in their separate college worlds.

Cecily von Ziegesar

As a teenager I read a lot of books. Books with lots of scary trends, things like nuclear weapons and overpopulation and global diseases, and I thought, 'Wouldn't it be great to write stories that showed people these problems and that we could do something about them.'

Jeffrey Skoll

I think when you get interested in antiques, the most frustrating thing is that books don't have enough photos. When you go to a flea market or garage sale, you see lots of things you've never seen before and you have no idea what the price is going to be or should be.

Judith Miller

My home has a split personality. Some of the rooms are very French antique. Think Aubusson rugs, turquoise ceramic jugs, sandbag pillows, and broken birdcages. The other half is very Aztec. Neon ikat fabric pillows, vintage books piled up to the ceiling, and shutters from Bali.

Poppy Delevingne

We live in the country, and I have a huge library there. When we go to London for the winter I never know which books to take. I never know what I am going to need. That's the only disadvantage.

Mordecai Richler

The power of the human spirit inspires me. Movies, books, stories, people, anything that reminds us that we are more than just this physical body and our capacity for love and courage can bend reality.

Caity Lotz

I'm a people person, very approachable. I go out every night, tons of functions. I love all facets of this industry... Music, film, TV, books, art. I love being around creative people.

Guy Oseary

While books provided me with some escape from the mental and physical horrors of my early life, they were unreliable. Many times the protagonists suffered terribly and then died at the end.

Sherrilyn Kenyon

The Pentagon can't even audit its own books. It doesn't even know where its money is going. And we refuse to have the tough forces go on the Pentagon so that at least they are efficient with the money they're spending.

Tom Coburn

Why do I do this every Sunday? Even the book reviews seem to be the same as last week's. Different books same reviews.

John Osborne

I'm fortunate that the books sell, but even more fortunate to live in Chatham, to be very happily married and to have, on the whole, a fairly clear conscience.

Bernard Cornwell

If you're creating something that has some sort of cultural currency - if the idea is getting out there - then that will probably yield money in some form, whether it's through selling art or selling books or being asked to give a lecture.

Shepard Fairey

At hotels, you are an actress. Absolutely. You can do what you want. Go where you want. I love my home too. But I love to arrive in a hotel. They have books, chocolate, food. I put things in the little refrigerator.

Sonia Rykiel

Until I read Anne Frank's diary, I had found books a literal escape from what could be the harsh reality around me. After I read the diary, I had a fresh way of viewing the both literature and the world. From then on, I found I was impatient with books that were not honest or that were trivial and frivolous.

Alexandra Fuller

I think there's a great difference in consciousness in that same way in that when we're young we read books for the story, for the excitement of the story - and there comes a

time when you realise that all stories are more or less the same story.

John McGahern

The technology that threatens to kill off books as we know them - the 'physical book,' a new phrase in our language - is also making the physical book capable of being more beautiful than books have been since the middle ages.

Art Spiegelman

Books have this function that help me to understand the work I've done, to wrap it up. Once it's done, fortunately, it doesn't mean there's closure.

Wolfgang Tillmans

I don't go to the beach. There is no value in going to the beach. If I did go I would probably read economics books.

Esther Duflo

There's been resistance to every new technology that's ever been introduced. When books came out hundreds of years ago, there were complaints that it would destroy the oral

tradition. Some of those fears were justified, but it didn't stop the rise of the written word. And books have proven to be incredibly useful.

Jeremy Stoppelman

I'm a fan of meeting readers face to face, at reader events, where we're able to sit down and take some time to talk. Too often, at regular book signings, I meet readers who have traveled six or eight hours to see me, and I'm unable to spend more than a few short minutes chatting with them as I sign books.

Suzanne Brockmann

Art needs to be socialised, and you need a lot of context to understand that, and that doesn't mean having read a few art history books.

Peter M. Brant

I can no more reread my own books than I can watch old home movies or look at snapshots of myself as a child. I wind up sitting on the floor, paralyzed by grief and nostalgia.

Francine Prose

To limit the press is to insult a nation; to prohibit reading of certain books is to declare the inhabitants to be either fools or slaves.

Claude Adrien Helvetius

Write comic books if you love comic books so much that you want to write them. Don't write them like movies. Comics can do a lot of things that movies can't do, and vice versa.

Grant Morrison

The marketplace for books when I entered the business shortly after World War II consisted of a thousand or so well stocked independent booksellers in major towns and cities supplemented by thousands of smaller shops that carried limited stocks of mostly current titles along with greeting cards, toys and so on.

Jason Epstein

Two more years were to go by before I knew anything about William Blake. Many years later, when his wife died, my godfather gave me the two books as a remembrance.

Laurence Housman

There are some beautiful books out there. But the ones that leave me cold are the ones where I feel - it's that postmodern thing - it's more experimentation with language than it is a deep compassionate falling into another human being's experience.

Andre Dubus III

The bailout of Fannie Mae is completely off the books. It's going to cost us hundreds of billions of dollars. Yet nobody is placing this in any type of column in accounting for federal debt.

Leonard Lance

No one bothered reading the books and understanding - and again, I'm not being high-falutin' about it - but I think our books are great literature with great metaphors of real life dealing with fears and hopes.

Avi Arad

When I was growing up the publishing world seemed so far away. When my mother wrote a book, she would look up

the address of publishers on the backs of the books she owned and send off her manuscript.

Kiran Desai

Probably I, like a lot of people, became a writer in imitation of or in homage to the books I enjoyed. When you're so captivated by something, you think, could I do that? Hmm, let me try.

Curtis Sittenfeld

Books don't exist unless you read them. And it's a two way process - you write the book as you read it and you fill in the gaps. You discover it and you put the marks together and without you doing it they're just marks.

Samuel West

I think the kind of unexpected I really love is when you open books and the actual way of writing is different and interesting. Like reading Virginia Woolf for the first time or Lawrence Durrell for the first time.

Lalla Ward

These 'mistakes' occur in my books for a reason. I have an agenda: I'm secretly trying to inspire kids to create their own stories and comics, and I don't want them to feel stifled by 'perfectionism.'

Dav Pilkey

My husband, Nick Chiles and I wrote a number of relationship books together, and what we found was that women were thirsty to hear directly from men.

Denene Millner

I found, through the process of doing 'The Perks of Being a Wallflower,' that I really love directing movies and I love writing books and so this will become the centerpiece of my career for the next ten or twenty years. Doing these adaptations.

Stephen Chbosky

When today's generation reads Jack's books or they listen to the music created by some of us, I believe that they see there is a different way of approaching today's life and today's sometimes seeming hopelessness that can provide answers.

David Amram

I don't want my books to exclude anyone, but if they have to, then I would rather they excluded the people who feel they are too smart for them!

Nick Hornby

Whether as victim, demon, or hero, the industrial worker of the past century filled the public imagination in books, movies, news stories, and even popular songs, putting a grimy human face on capitalism while dramatizing the social changes and conflicts it brought.

George Packer

A collection of good books, with a soul to it in the shape of a librarian, becomes a vitalized power among the impulses by which the world goes on to improvement.

Justin Winsor

Dark books do appeal to kids because they have nice, sheltered lives - and they also appeal to children who are going through pretty hard times themselves.

Melissa de la Cruz

The architecture for 'Paladin' - given that it's at least three books, with the possibility of more - turned out to be bigger than anything I've ever created, with multiple levels of reality, interlocking mysteries and a terabyte of time frame.

Mark Frost

I was always a really big fan of R. L. Stine and the 'Goosebumps' T.V. series and the 'Goosebumps' books.

Dylan Minnette

The expectation was that 'True Confessions' would be my first published book, but that didn't happen. After it was rejected by every publisher in New York and Canada, I shoved it in a closet and went on to write and publish my next three books.

Rachel Gibson

I grew up on Stephen King, reading the books. I love the small town, 1950s feel to it, that nostalgia, and that old America. What happens when something weird starts happening to all these people, something other-worldly, something demonic?

Alexander Koch

I don't think with any book you get used to people falling in love with the story. It's been incredible just to realize your books are being read. It's a pretty amazing feeling.

Jennifer Armentrout

I don't keep any copy of my books around... they would embarass me. When I finish writing my books, I kick them in the belly, and have done with them.

Ludwig Bemelmans

I created 'Captain Underpants' when I was in the second grade. I was constantly getting in trouble for being the class clown, so my teacher sent me out into the hallway to punish me. It was there in the hall that I began drawing 'Captain Underpants'. Soon I was making my own comic books about him.

Dav Pilkey

It gives me a huge buzz when people say they've enjoyed my books, because this grew out of a hobby, and it's an absolute passion, and it's lovely when I get feedback.

Alison Weir

One of my books, 'Rain Falling on My Face,' earned me the 39th Edogawa Ranpo prize. It's a very prestigious literary prize in Japan, mostly for mysteries and thrillers.

Natsuo Kirino

I like the 'Cirque du Freak' books - 'Tunnel of Blood' by Darren Shan. They're set in England. It's about vampires.

Jamie Waylett

I always love writing the third book in a series because you get to tie up all the threads that you put out in the first two books. You finally let people know what really happens and reveal all the secrets and bring certain characters together.

Trudi Canavan

A lot of the time writers are just sponges... for what's around them, and so books are helpful for focusing your mind and literally putting it into words.

Marcus Mumford

I have on my bookshelf a series of books with opposite titles: 'The Alpha Strategy' and the 'Omega Strategy'; 'Asia Rising' and 'Asia Falling'; 'Free to Choose' and 'Free to Lose'; 'How to Win Friends and Influence People' and 'How to Lose Friends and Alienate People.' Visitors love the collection.

Mark Skousen

There are still some people out there who believe comic books are nothing more than, well, comic books. But the true cognoscenti know graphic novels are - at their best - an amazing blend of art literature and the theater of the mind.

John Ridley

The world's entire scientific and cultural heritage, published over centuries in books and journals, is increasingly being digitized and locked up by a handful of private corporations.

Aaron Swartz

Basically, books were a luxury item before the printing press.

Nate Silver

I live on the other side of Copernicus and Galileo; I can no longer conceive of God as sort of above the sky, looking down and keeping record books.

John Shelby Spong

Read, read, read. Read good books. You will strengthen your understanding of story. Your vocabulary will be the richer for it.

Carmen Agra Deedy

If you think you have it tough, read history books.

Bill Maher

As a strong supporter of our 2nd Amendment rights, I believe tougher enforcement of our nation's existing gun laws must be done before any more laws are enacted and put on the books.

Jeff Miller

Had I not had children of my own, I would have never written books for children, nor would I have been capable of doing so.

Roald Dahl

A well-designed home has to be very comfortable. I can't stand the aesthetes, the minimal thing. I can't live that way. My home has to be filled with stuff - mostly paintings, sculpture, my fish lamps, cardboard furniture, lots of books.

Frank Gehry

Laws against homosexual behavior should remain on the books.

Orson Scott Card

Young men should prove theorems, old men should write books.

G. H. Hardy

This is what I believe is most important: getting good books into the hands of kids - books that will make them want to say, 'Wow, that was great. Give me another one to

read.'

James Patterson

The Sistine Chapel is an extraordinary work of education - it lays out all the early books of the Bible.

Peter Greenaway

Never lend books, for no one ever returns them; the only books I have in my library are books that other folks have left me.

Anatole France

Life being very short, and the quiet hours of it few, we ought to waste none of them in reading valueless books.

John Ruskin

My books are all fantastically sentimental.

Chuck Palahniuk

By burning Luther's books you may rid your bookshelves

of him, but you will not rid men's minds of him.

Desiderius Erasmus

No, I got a GED in my 30s. My kids know that I never stop learning, and they know I love reading. I have books overflowing everywhere. I am current on today's events and I read the paper every day, and we talk about it, so they see that appetite.

Michael J. Fox

I love books, and all the best ones are people analysing their own emotions. You can learn from that.

John Lydon

Next, in importance to books are their titles.

Frank Crane

Television and comic books are, and continue to be, probably the biggest influence in my life. It's the biggest influence on everybody's life.

Gene Simmons

I realise how important it is to use the time I have. I respect people who want to do that by watching television. I happen to want to read books. But I know I can't read all the books or watch all the movies in one lifetime.

Viggo Mortensen

I admire the world of the books and the characters that she's created, but I'm not an addict of Harry Potter. I don't feel possessive about it.

Ralph Fiennes

For many years I had heard about an underworld consisting of people who act out a vampire fantasy while I was living in New York. Fortunately for me there are also several books on the phenomena.

James Patterson

It's our job - as parents, grandparents, aunts, uncles - to find books our kids are going to like.

James Patterson

I love to read. I have a Kindle, and it's nice to be able to download books that people refer.

Kellan Lutz

My mom says: 'Why aren't you a doctor?' and I'm like, 'I am a doctor!' and she's all, 'No, I mean a real doctor.' She reads my books, but she says they give her a headache.

Brian Greene

How could I make a little book, when I have seen enough to make a dozen large books?

John James Audubon

I often reread books I have written.

Taylor Caldwell

I want to know if I look up a whole lot of books about some form of cancer that that's not going to get to my insurance company and I'm going to find my insurance premium is going to go up by 5% because they've figured I'm looking at those books.

Tim Berners-Lee

There are too many books I haven't read, too many places I haven't seen, too many memories I haven't kept long enough.

Irwin Shaw

I gauge success in years, not weeks. The weekend box-office approach to book launches is short sighted and encourages crappy books.

Timothy Ferriss

When you write non-fiction, you sit down at your desk with a pile of notebooks, newspaper clippings, and books and you research and put a book together the way you would a jigsaw puzzle.

Janine di Giovanni

When my generation grew up, our only sources of knowledge were books, teachers, parents and friends. The encyclopedia was an item of luxury. We faced big limits in what we could learn, where we could be and who we could reach.

Vivek Wadhwa

I loved reading Roald Dahl when I was young but I had forgotten a lot about the books. I read the 'BFG' on the iPad the other day and it was so interesting to see his descriptions of clothes and places.

Frank Lampard

For books are more than books, they are the life, the very heart and core of ages past, the reason why men worked and died, the essence and quintessence of their lives.

Amy Lowell

I've read a lot of bad books. I used to review books for a living, and when you're a reviewer you read tons of terrible books.

John Green

You need to put easy, nice, tranquil thoughts in your head before you go to bed. You know what I do? I read metaphysical books. The good stuff stays in your brain once you go under.

Cristina Saralegui

I actually really suck at naming books, so lots of years ago, readers were sending in their ideas for titles, and what we realized is that they were smarter than us. So we thought, Hey, go for it. So now we have a contest every year.

Janet Evanovich

I knew that if I wrote a new book every six months or every year, if I continued to read great books, eventually I would write something worthy of publication. I understood I might be in my forties or my fifties or even my sixties, but I felt confident that it would happen.

Augusten Burroughs

The homes I like the best are totally occupied, busy, and useful, whether it's a tiny little house or a great big one. Rarely do you find a great big house that's used in a good way. So I prefer smaller spaces that are full of books, full of things that people are doing.

Martha Stewart

I had a briefcase at one point, but it was a kind of 1980s New Wave briefcase. It was made of some kind of cardboard and it had metal hinges. It was kind of faux

industrial looking, and I used to carry my books in it rather than a backpack. I didn't want to have normal student accoutrements.

Jeffrey Eugenides

But I like all the books. You've got to read them all to get the complete Harry Potter experience.

Rupert Grint

In my books, women often solve the problem. Even if the woman is not the hero, she's a strong character. She does change the plot. She'll often rescue the male character from some situation.

Ken Follett

I spend a lot of time preparing. I think a lot about what I want to do. I have prep books, little notebooks in which I write everything down before a sitting. Otherwise I would forget my ideas.

Helmut Newton

I'm a big 'Star Wars' fan and grew up watching the movies.

I read all the books and have read 'Star Wars' fiction that went between the newest trilogy and the original trilogy and it was part of my childhood.

Jared Padalecki

I always say that the characters in Jane Austen's original books are rather like zombies because they live in this bubble of immense wealth and privilege and no matter what's going on around them they have a singular purpose to maintain their rank and to impress others.

Seth Grahame-Smith

I think it's a fallacy to say that a good book sells itself. It doesn't happen. I'm a voracious reader and I can give you a long list of books which should have been best sellers but they aren't. How can you buy a book if you haven't heard of it?

Amish Tripathi

I love my lecture tours. I get up onstage. I have my stack of books and a glass of water and a microphone. No podium, no distance between me and the audience, and I just talk to people and get all excited and tell a lot of jokes, and sing some songs, and read from my work and remind people how powerful they are and how beautiful they are.

Suzan-Lori Parks

When I was a kid, there were these great comic books called 'Tales From The Crypt' and 'The Vault of Horror.' They were gruesome. I discovered them in the barbershop and thought they were fabulous.

R. L. Stine

Good dreams are better than films or books.

Alison Goldfrapp

What's funny about that is when I was writing Twilight just for myself and not thinking of it as a book, I was not thinking about publishing, and yet at the same time I was casting it in my head. Because when I read books, I see them very visually.

Stephenie Meyer

I have to admit that I am really partial to the look and feel of a book. I have been that way my entire life. I like the weight, look, and feel of a book. I enjoy turning the pages, and frequently scan the spines of my many books on the wall, each title a reminder of the stored information and

creative thoughts contained therein.

Al Seckel

As readers can probably tell from my books, I love the outdoors.

Sharon Creech

There's something about each of my books that I'm really proud of, and there's something about each of my books that I cringe over.

Margaret Haddix

In 2002, Google began an ambitious project to digitize every book in the world. It was intended as a search project: type in a query, and Google would show you snippets. They asked university libraries for books, which they would scan for free. At Harvard we didn't permit them to take works under copyright, but other libraries gave them everything.

Robert Darnton

I've always thought Harper Lee might have made a great

decision. Much as you'd like to have more books by her, there's something about just one that's kind of mysterious and nice. On the other hand, the New York gossip about me was that I'd never write another book. So I thought, 'Well, I will then.'

Charles Frazier

In real life, people are integrated into society. That's what happens in my books as well. Minor characters don't just walk in and spout lines, they interact and have an effect on the events. It's not an isolated universe.

Stieg Larsson

I read a lot of fantasy. I adored 'Anne of Green Gables'. But my favourite books as a child were probably Laura Ingalls Wilder's 'Little House' series, about a pioneer family in the mid-19th-century American west. I often thought of them as I was writing 'The Last Runaway'.

Tracy Chevalier

Whites were the winners, blacks were the losers, we wrote the history books, and they didn't feature.

Phillip Noyce

Books have become products, like cereal or perfume or deodorant.

Alexandra Ripley

I've always been interested in science - one of my favourite books is James Watson's 'Molecular Biology of the Gene.'

Bill Gates

There is no author whose books I look forward to more than Vaclav Smil.

Bill Gates

The multitude of books is making us ignorant.

Voltaire

The proper study of mankind is books.

Aldous Huxley

I can't consciously explain how people feel after reading my books. All is too personal.

Paulo Coelho

I read whatever is put in front of me. I gobble up books.

Kara Hayward

I think I would like to write screenplays, books, really anything.

Kara Hayward

If I have to go to New York or something, I'll bring my books and read and do homework. It's not really a big deal.

Kara Hayward

Books are not made for furniture, but there is nothing else that so beautifully furnishes a house.

Henry Ward Beecher

There are three schoolmasters for everybody that will

employ them - the senses, intelligent companions, and books.

Henry Ward Beecher

In books lies the soul of the whole past time.

Thomas Carlyle

The true university of these days is a collection of books.

Thomas Carlyle

History books that contain no lies are extremely dull.

Anatole France

The books that everybody admires are those that nobody reads.

Anatole France

Electronic books are junk.

Ray Bradbury

All books are divisible into two classes, the books of the hour, and the books of all time.

John Ruskin

Publishers like a good buzz, and negative responses sell books just as well as positive ones.

Richard Dawkins

I get angry about stuff, I get very emotionally intense about stuff and that's how I get it out - with books, with the band, on my own onstage, but it's always kind of a wail.

Henry Rollins

I wouldn't get nearly as many books written if I lived in New York. The Columbia Gorge is fantastic. When the sun shines, I just want to be outdoors.

Chuck Palahniuk

An author who speaks about their own books is almost as bad as a mother who speaks about her own children.

Benjamin Disraeli

There are people out there who will not read books, but somehow they'll read my books.

Chuck Palahniuk

I write in a noisy, distracting world so the books can be read there.

Chuck Palahniuk

If you read a lot of books you are considered well read. But if you watch a lot of TV, you're not considered well viewed.

Lily Tomlin

When you've written 10 books and have six on the New York Times best-seller list - and four have been No. 1 - I think you have a right to be a member of Congress.

Marianne Williamson

The earliest books in the New Testament to be written were

the Epistles, not the Gospels. It's almost as though Saint Paul and others who wrote the Epistles weren't that interested in whether Jesus was real.

Richard Dawkins

Books that you carry to the fire, and hold readily in your hand, are most useful after all.

Samuel Johnson

If anything I try to write something that would be more difficult to film. I tend to see film as competition and would like instead to do what books do best.

Chuck Palahniuk

My first four books, from 'Fight Club' to 'Choke,' dealt with personal identity issues. The crises the narrators found themselves in were generated by themselves.

Chuck Palahniuk

Books are so cheap and easy to get that people don't bother stealing them, which is the essential rule of piracy that the music business learned much too late.

Tucker Max

Who I am, what I am, is the culmination of a lifetime of reading, a lifetime of stories. And there are still so many more books to read. I'm a work in progress.

Sarah Addison Allen

Isn't it strange that I who have written only unpopular books should be such a popular fellow?

Albert Einstein

The books that the world calls immoral are books that show the world its own shame.

Oscar Wilde

All good books have one thing in common - they are truer than if they had really happened.

Ernest Hemingway

I write books because I have always been fascinated by stories and language, and because I love thinking about

what makes people tick. Writing a story... 'The Giver' or any other... is simply an exploration of the nature of behavior: why people do what they do, how it affects others, how we change and grow, and what decisions we make along the way.

Lois Lowry

Books constitute capital. A library book lasts as long as a house, for hundreds of years. It is not, then, an article of mere consumption but fairly of capital, and often in the case of professional men, setting out in life, it is their only capital.

Thomas Jefferson

I usually give a book 40 pages. If it doesn't grab me by then, adios. With young adult books, you can usually tell by Page 4 if it's worth the time. The author establishes the conflict early, sometimes in the first sentence. The themes of hope, family, friendship and overcoming hardship appeal to most everyone.

Regina Brett

You know, I don't only play for the record books.

Roger Federer

I love comic books and I love anime.

Samuel L. Jackson

My books are about ordinary people, like you, me, people on the street, people who really have an expectation of reasonable happiness in life, want their life to have a sense of security and predictability, who want to belong to something bigger than them, who want love and affection in their life, who want a good future for the children.

Khaled Hosseini

Now my only income is a few royalty cheques from my books.

Bobby Fischer

Every book you pick up has its own lesson or lessons, and quite often the bad books have more to teach than the good ones.

Stephen King

Back in my days as a children's book editor, my superiors

caught on to the fact that teenagers were using the Internet to gossip about each other, and thought it might be nifty to develop a series of books about an anonymous high-school blogger who gossips about her classmates. The concept was passed on to me.

Cecily von Ziegesar

One day I was in Starbucks going through one of my books on accounting, and this beautiful young woman came up to me and said, 'My accounting book is different from yours.' Her name was Joyce, she had a background in finance and administration and ran a surgery center. Within a short time, we were married.

David Schweikert

There are worse crimes than burning books. One of them is not reading them.

Ray Bradbury

Whatever hardships there have been in my life I still live in a very privileged position. Fear is not knowing where your next meal is coming from. Fear is seeing a child get hurt. Fear is watching someone you love waste away. Fear is knowing you are going to die yourself. But there's no fear in what I do. I write books.

James Frey

My books are like water; those of the great geniuses are wine. (Fortunately) everybody drinks water.

Mark Twain

It is an awfully sad misconception that librarians simply check books in and out. The library is the heart of a school, and without a librarian, it is but an empty shell.

Jarrett J. Krosoczka

Heart is what drives us and determines our fate. That is what I need for my characters in my books: a passionate heart. I need mavericks, dissidents, adventurers, outsiders and rebels, who ask questions, bend the rules and take risks.

Isabel Allende

The remedy for life's broken pieces is not classes, workshops or books. Don't try to heal the broken pieces. Just forgive.

Iyanla Vanzant

I think there are so many books out there written on relationships and romance that women are the authors of. How can women know exactly how men think? And there are so many guys out there with relationship books who are just not telling the truth. They have shaded parts.

Steve Harvey

The white man made the mistake of letting me read his history books. He made the mistake of teaching me that Patrick Henry was a patriot and George Washington - wasn't nothing non-violent about old Pat or George Washington.

Malcolm X

We are motivated by a keen desire for praise, and the better a man is the more he is inspired by glory. The very philosophers themselves, even in those books which they write in contempt of glory, inscribe their names.

Marcus Tullius Cicero

Whatever happened to books? Suddenly everybody's talking about these 100-hour movies called 'Breaking Bad'. People are talking about TV the same way they used to talk

about novels back in the 1980s. I like to think I hang out with some pretty smart people, but all they talk about is 'Breaking Bad.'

Douglas Coupland

Books are like imprisoned souls till someone takes them down from a shelf and frees them.

Samuel Butler

Books and marriage go ill together.

Moliere

Books let us into their souls and lay open to us the secrets of our own.

William Hazlitt

I like to play football, read some books, study.

Andrew Luck

Well, now that he's finished one building, he'll go write

four books about it.

Frank Lloyd Wright

Upon books the collective education of the race depends; they are the sole instruments of registering, perpetuating and transmitting thought.

Harry S Truman

I never thought, in my lifetime, that you'd be able to watch movies, read books and listen to music from a phone, but I guess the technology of tomorrow is here today.

Dolly Parton

Books are the money of Literature, but only the counters of Science.

Thomas Huxley

Cooking, decorating, diet/self-help and gardening books are guilty pleasures and useful time fillers.

Hillary Clinton

I regret all of my books.

Zora Neale Hurston

There was a time when the world acted on books; now books act on the world.

Joseph Joubert

I remember being in the public library and my jaw just aching as I looked around at all those books I wanted to read. There just wasn't time enough to read everything I wanted to read.

Charles Kuralt

I was very interested in vaudeville. It was the only sort of discipline that was a five-minute act on stage, which is what I really enjoyed and saw myself doing. And I bought books on it.

Steve Martin

My thought has been shaped by books; my desires by pictures.

Mason Cooley

Master books, but do not let them master you. Read to live, not live to read.

Edward G. Bulwer-Lytton

I like writing. I get cranky when I can't. Yes, I write books back to back, and I work very hard on them.

Terry Pratchett

Books, like proverbs, receive their chief value from the stamp and esteem of the ages through which they have passed.

J. Paul Getty

Books choose their authors; the act of creation is not entirely a rational and conscious one.

Salman Rushdie

One sheds one's sicknesses in books - repeats and presents again one's emotions, to be master of them.

D. H. Lawrence

I do like books on anatomy. I have to say I'm an amateur physician, I guess.

Tom Waits

Money is an unavoidable consequence, but it isn't the reason I write; if it was, I wouldn't have written any of the YA books, because advances in that field are small compared to what I'd got now for an 'adult' DW.

Terry Pratchett

Read much, but not many books.

Gustave Flaubert

The thing is, 'Discworld' had been going on for a very long time, and I've written children's books as well. Usually when people have a really big series they franchise it, which I thought is a bit of a no-no, so I thought what I'd do is I'd franchise it to myself.

Terry Pratchett

Men do not understand books until they have a certain

amount of life, or at any rate no man understands a deep book, until he has seen and lived at least part of its contents.

Ezra Pound

I write books I'd enjoy reading, I'm the reader standing behind my shoulder.

Salman Rushdie

It is shallow people who think beauty is frivolous or excessive. If you are bringing beauty and god, you are enriching the country. Rice feeds the body, books feed the mind, beauty feeds the soul. It is one thing I can really be proud of and stand tall in the world.

Imelda Marcos

Books serve to show a man that those original thoughts of his aren't very new at all.

Abraham Lincoln

Nature and books belong to the eyes that see them.

Ralph Waldo Emerson

I am not a fan of books.

Kanye West

I'm the biggest nerd - I love comic books and stuff like that! I don't have any friends who are actresses. I only had one girlfriend when I was growing up. Most of my friends were boys. I was such a tomboy. I enjoyed doing guy things.

Megan Fox

Nine-tenths of tactics are certain, and taught in books: but the irrational tenth is like the kingfisher flashing across the pool, and that is the test of generals.

T. E. Lawrence

Kids don't even read comic books anymore. They've got more important things to do - like video games.

Ang Lee

The books I love most are the ones that combine some sort of gripping story with really beautiful or stylish writing.

Some of my favorites are 'The Road' by Cormac McCarthy, 'The Virgin Suicides' by Jeffrey Eugenides, 'The Interpreter of Maladies' by Jhumpa Lahiri, and 'Blindness' by Jose Saramago.

Karen Thompson Walker

The Bible is worth all the other books which have ever been printed.

Patrick Henry

The younger generation is surrounded by the Internet, apps, and video games. But somehow, my books make them read.

Chetan Bhagat

I've only wanted paper and beautiful colors. It was my dream, and it still is my dream. And books. They're all I need, and the rest I can do without.

Karl Lagerfeld

It had been startling and disappointing to me to find out that story books had been written by people, that books

were not natural wonders, coming of themselves like grass.

Eudora Welty

Books are the quietest and most constant of friends; they are the most accessible and wisest of counselors, and the most patient of teachers.

Charles William Eliot

Name the book that made the biggest impression on you. I bet you read it before you hit puberty. In the time I've got left, I intend to write artistic books - for kids - because they're still open to new ideas.

Gary Paulsen

There are books of which the backs and covers are by far the best parts.

Charles Dickens

Half of my library are old books because I like seeing how people thought about their world at their time. So that I don't get bigheaded about something we just discovered and I can be humble about where we might go next.

Because you can see who got stuff right and most of the people who got stuff wrong.

Neil deGrasse Tyson

The brilliance of Max Brooks is that he always quotes authorities at the back of his books that never existed. Like a Russian professor he made up that validates a story or character.

Mel Brooks

I believe we should spend less time worrying about the quantity of books children read and more time introducing them to quality books that will turn them on to the joy of reading and turn them into lifelong readers.

James Patterson

My best investment, as cliched as this sounds, is the money I've spent developing myself, via books, workshops and coaching. Leadership begins within, and to have a better career, start by building a better you.

Robin S. Sharma

When I was growing up, if there was a Young Adult section of my town's library, I missed it. I wandered right from 'The Babysitter's Club' over to Stephen King. His books were big and fat and they seemed important. I eventually worked my way through most of the shelf, but 'It' is the one that stuck with me.

Erin Morgenstern

Censorship ends in logical completeness when nobody is allowed to read any books except the books that nobody reads.

George Bernard Shaw

This will never be a civilized country until we spend more money for books than we do for chewing gum.

Elbert Hubbard

I know many books which have bored their readers, but I know of none which has done real evil.

Voltaire

I've only written one science-fiction book: 'Fahrenheit 451.'

That book is a book based on real facts and my hatred of people who destroy books.

Ray Bradbury

The act of writing is a way of tricking yourself into revealing something that you would never consciously put into the world. Sometimes I'm shocked by the deeply personal things I've put into books without realizing it.

Chuck Palahniuk

Men have had every advantage of us in telling their own story. Education has been theirs in so much higher a degree; the pen has been in their hands. I will not allow books to prove anything.

Jane Austen

You are welcome to your intellectual pastimes and books and art and newspapers; welcome, too, to your bars and your whisky that only makes me ill. Here am I in the forest, quite content.

Knut Hamsun

My only books were woman's looks, and folly's all they've taught me.

Thomas Moore

I spent my first two years at a small all-male college in Virginia called Hampden-Sydney. That was like going to college 120 years ago. The languages, a year of rhetoric, all of the great books, Western Man courses, stuff like that.

Stephen Colbert

What progress we are making. In the Middle Ages they would have burned me. Now they are content with burning my books.

Sigmund Freud

Books are the bees which carry the quickening pollen from one to another mind.

James Russell Lowell

He who studies books alone will know how things ought to be, and he who studies men will know how they are.

Charles Caleb Colton

The cliche of the nerdy kid who doesn't go outside and just plays games is completely untrue. And it's also true for the nerdy kid who studies comic books and turns into this genius, and it is also true for the nerdy kid who listens to every nerdy thing that Led Zeppelin put out. That kind of obsession in a 16-year-old is not ugly. It's beautiful.

Penn Jillette

Books are slow, books are quiet. The Internet is fast and loud.

Jonathan Safran Foer

Read a lot - poems, prose, stories, newspapers, anything. Read books and poems that you think you will like and some that you think might not be for you. You might be surprised.

Michael Morpurgo

Through books and photographs, I saw a world that was not my own - and I realized that there was another world. That's why I'm concerned about education, because it helps our children see other worlds.

Bette Midler

I always figured there would be a kid audience and an adult audience, and there is. That's true for 'Hunger Games' and 'Twilight' and 'Harry Potter.' And 'Maximum Ride,' for sure. In particular what happens is a lot of parents share the books with their kids, and the mom has read it, and the kids, and they talk about it.

James Patterson

I often feel I'm a disappointment to people because they expect me to be the guy in the books. When I sit next to someone at a dinner party I can see they expect me to be quick and witty, and I'm not at all.

Bill Bryson

There's a variety and depth to the song topics I get to write about in children's music and books: being able to write about things I wouldn't normally write about, like a disappointing pancake, or monsters or opposite day is really different than writing about heartbreak and relationships.

Lisa Loeb

People say I don't write books, I make Christmas presents.

Bryce Courtenay

I never really had any close friends in India, and I felt a
terrible loneliness and isolation for many years.
Westernized Indians don't like my books and I tend not to
like westernized Indians - so we're quits.

Ruth Prawer Jhabvala

Ideas are only lethal if you suppress and don't discuss them.
Ignorance is not bliss, it's stupid. Banning books shows you
don't trust your kids to think and you don't trust yourself to
be able to talk to them.

Anna Quindlen

I took every chance I could to meet with U.S. soldiers. I
talked with them and read the books they gave me about
the war. I decided I needed to return to my country and join
with them - active duty soldiers and Vietnam Veterans in
particular - to try and end the war.

Jane Fonda

My heart goes out to victims and survivors of the Hurricane Katrina tragedy and to their families. This disaster will go down in history books as one of the largest natural disasters in U.S. history.

Ellen Tauscher

I like books that aren't just lovely but that have memories in themselves. Just like playing a song, picking up a book again that has memories can take you back to another place or another time.

Emma Watson

One whose knowledge is confined to books and whose wealth is in the possession of others, can use neither his knowledge nor wealth when the need for them arises.

Chanakya

A home without books is a body without soul.

Marcus Tullius Cicero

We go to school to learn to work hard for money. I write books and create products that teach people how to have

money work hard for them.

Robert Kiyosaki

I still have my unemployment books and I remember when I worked for the sanitation department and the post office.

Denzel Washington

Prolonged, indiscriminate reviewing of books is a quite exceptionally thankless, irritating and exhausting job. It not only involves praising trash but constantly inventing reactions towards books about which one has no spontaneous feeling whatever.

George Orwell

I grew up thinking that I would become a fighter pilot and was fascinated by aircrafts as I had grown up around that. But my father encouraged me to not become an Air Force person, given the varied interests I had, be it books, movies, sports or fighter flying.

Kapil Sharma

It is a good thing for an uneducated man to read books of

quotations.

Winston Churchill

Books are as useful to a stupid person as a mirror is useful to a blind person.

Chanakya

After all manner of professors have done their best for us, the place we are to get knowledge is in books. The true university of these days is a collection of books.

Albert Camus

I was teased if I brought my books home. I would take a paper bag to the library and put the books in the bag and bring them home. Not that I was that concerned about them teasing me - because I would hit them in a heartbeat. But I felt a little ashamed, having books.

Walter Dean Myers

The tree I had in the garden as a child, my beech tree, I used to climb up there and spend hours. I took my homework up there, my books, I went up there if I was sad,

and it just felt very good to be up there among the green leaves and the birds and the sky.

Jane Goodall

We're taught Lord Acton's axiom: all power corrupts, absolute power corrupts absolutely. I believed that when I started these books, but I don't believe it's always true any more. Power doesn't always corrupt. Power can cleanse. What I believe is always true about power is that power always reveals.

Robert Caro

The impulse to dream was slowly beaten out of me by experience. Now it surged up again and I hungered for books, new ways of looking and seeing.

Richard Wright

With paper printed books, you have certain freedoms. You can acquire the book anonymously by paying cash, which is the way I always buy books. I never use a credit card. I don't identify to any database when I buy books. Amazon takes away that freedom.

Richard Stallman

What we become depends on what we read after all of the professors have finished with us. The greatest university of all is a collection of books.

Thomas Carlyle

I couldn't live a week without a private library - indeed, I'd part with all my furniture and squat and sleep on the floor before I'd let go of the 1500 or so books I possess.

H. P. Lovecraft

A house without books is like a room without windows. No man has a right to bring up his children without surrounding them with books, if he has the means to buy them.

Horace Mann

When you're writing a book, with people in it as opposed to animals, it is no good having people who are ordinary, because they are not going to interest your readers at all. Every writer in the world has to use the characters that have something interesting about them, and this is even more true in children's books.

Roald Dahl

As far as I knew white women were never lonely, except in
books. White men adored them, Black men desired them
and Black women worked for them.

Maya Angelou

Books were my pass to personal freedom. I learned to read
at age three, and soon discovered there was a whole world
to conquer that went beyond our farm in Mississippi.

Oprah Winfrey

But more wonderful than the lore of old men and the lore of
books is the secret lore of ocean.

H. P. Lovecraft

Jewish villages were built in the place of Arab villages.
You do not even know the names of these Arab villages,
and I do not blame you because geography books no longer
exist.

Moshe Dayan

I believe in communication; books communicate ideas and make bridges between people.

Jeanette Winterson

I hate homework. I hate it more now than I did when I was the one lugging textbooks and binders back and forth from school. The hour my children are seated at the kitchen table, their books spread out before them, the crumbs of their after-school snack littering the table, is without a doubt the worst hour of my day.

Ayelet Waldman

I'm totally into new age and self-help books. I used to work in a bookstore and that's the section they gave me, and I got way into it. I just loved the power of positive thinking, letting yourself go.

Jason Mraz

The reason is that till date, in spite of advances in information technology and strategies of information, the written word in the form of books still remains one of humanity's most enduring legacies.

Ibrahim Babangida

The bastard form of mass culture is humiliated repetition...
always new books, new programs, new films, news items,
but always the same meaning.

Roland Barthes

I have had fans make me the big picture collages of the
photo books; I have had fans send me birthday cakes... sing
to me on my voicemail. I have had fans flash me. I have
had older fans give me their bras and underwear onstage.

Sean Combs

Getting close to books, and spending time by myself, I was
obliged to think about things I would never have thought
about if I was busy romping around with a brother and
sister.

Shelby Foote

I think instead writers and publishers and readers need to
go to the places where people are, and make the argument
that there is great value to the quiet, contemplative process
of reading a novel, that reading great books carefully offers
pleasures and consolations that no iPad app ever can.

John Green

Other people are talking about writing books about my life, or about some of the things I've done. I find it strange, but I also feel it's my life and my story, and I guess I better be the one to get it on paper the way it actually happened.

Chris Kyle

We do not need to proselytise either by our speech or by our writing. We can only do so really with our lives. Let our lives be open books for all to study.

Mahatma Gandhi

Many good sayings are to be found in holy books, but merely reading them will not make one religious.

Ramakrishna

Books are the blessed chloroform of the mind.

Oswald Chambers

The advice of the elders to young men is very apt to be as

unreal as a list of the hundred best books.

Oliver Wendell Holmes, Jr.

Not enough books focus on how a culture responds to radically new ideas or discovery. Especially in the biography genre, they tend to focus on all the sordid details in the life of the person who made the discovery. I find this path to be voyeuristic but not enlightening.

Neil deGrasse Tyson

Books can capture injustices in a way that stays with you and makes you want to do something about them. That's why they are so powerful.

Malala Yousafzai

Because it's so easy to medicate our need for self-worth by pandering to win followers, 'likes' and view counts, social media have become the metier of choice for many people who might otherwise channel that energy into books, music or art - or even into their own Web ventures.

Neil Strauss

I like motivational books, because I like the go-getting American spirit - your destiny is in your own hands, life is what you make it, don't accept your limitations, jump before you're pushed, leap before you look.

Louise Mensch

You've really got to start hitting the books because it's no joke out here.

Harper Lee

Ultimately, a great thriller is a roller coaster ride. I like to think that's a promise I have never failed to keep, and one that I'd say has served my books well.

James Patterson

My favorite books are the ones that make me smile for hours after reading them. I want that for my readers, for the sweetness to linger. Sort of like chocolate, but without the calories.

Sarah Addison Allen

Avoid demonizing television, computer games, and new

technologies. Electronic media may compete for kids' attention, but we're not going to get kids reading by badmouthing other entertainment. Admit that TV and games can do things books can't.

Jon Scieszka

I like to give people novels I think they would like, on no particular occasion - just when we're in a bookstore together. I like to receive reference books on my birthday.

Daniel Handler

I wanted to go into prison and come out a better person - mentally, physically. So, I read a lot of books, got my GED while I was in there, and worked out every day. Strong body, strong mind.

Ja Rule

Movies can't ruin books. They can only ruin movies.

S. E. Hinton

My books are always about somebody who is taken from aloneness and isolation - often elevated loneliness - to

community. It may be a denigrated community that is filthy and poor, but they are not alone; they are with people.

Chuck Palahniuk

I spend my happiest hours in reading Vedantic books. They are to me like the light of the morning, like the pure air of the mountains - so simple, so true, if once understood.

Max Muller

Today's public figures can no longer write their own speeches or books, and there is some evidence that they can't read them either.

Gore Vidal

My advice is this. For Christ's sake, don't write a book that is suitable for a kid of 12 years old, because the kids who read who are 12 years old are reading books for adults. I read all of the James Bond books when I was about 11, which was approximately the right time to read James Bond books.

Terry Pratchett

I know that books seem like the ultimate thing that's made by one person, but that's not true. Every reading of a book is a collaboration between the reader and the writer who are making the story up together.

John Green

I've actually not read any books on time management.

Elon Musk

Nobody's favorite movie is some dark, dysfunctional slasher story. Everybody's favorite song is a sentimental song. So why all of a sudden is it bad to be sentimental in books?

Mitch Albom

Read. Read. Read. Just don't read one type of book. Read different books by various authors so that you develop different styles.

R. L. Stine

One of the most memorable things I hear is when someone tells me that my books got a reluctant reader to read.

Suzanne Collins

I didn't become a good writer until I learned how to rewrite. And I don't just mean fixing spelling and adding a comma. I rewrite each of my books five or six times, and each time I change huge portions of the story.

Louis Sachar

The Taliban's acts of cultural vandalism - the most infamous being the destruction of the giant Bamiyan Buddhas - had a devastating effect on Afghan culture and the artistic scene. The Taliban burned countless films, VCRs, music tapes, books, and paintings. They jailed filmmakers, musicians, painters, and sculptors.

Khaled Hosseini

I do a lot of research. For 'I Am Legend', I did a lot of research about survivors. If everybody is dead around you, how you can keep surviving. I went to the bookstore and found psychiatry books about survivors from the Holocaust.

Alice Braga

I think to be writer you have to enjoy being alone. I was a loner as a teenager and was always drawn to characters in books and films who were at the fringes.

Markus Zusak

Whether I'm at the office, at home, or on the road, I always have a stack of books I'm looking forward to reading.

Bill Gates

I don't mind saying, you know, that I don't take a salary from the church, and God has blessed me with more money than I could imagine from my books.

Joel Osteen

Who has fully realized that history is not contained in thick books but lives in our very blood?

Carl Jung

From your parents you learn love and laughter and how to put one foot before the other. But when books are opened you discover that you have wings.

Helen Hayes

It is from books that wise people derive consolation in the troubles of life.

Victor Hugo

Buying books would be a good thing if one could also buy the time to read them in: but as a rule the purchase of books is mistaken for the appropriation of their contents.

Arthur Schopenhauer

The real war will never get in the books.

Walt Whitman

All that I know about my life, it seems, I have learned in books.

Jean-Paul Sartre

Without words, without writing and without books there would be no history, there could be no concept of humanity.

Hermann Hesse

Surely the immutable laws of the universe can teach more impressive and exalted lessons than the holy books of all the religions on earth.

Elizabeth Cady Stanton

Outside books, we avoid colorful characters.

Mason Cooley

I think when people mean that Discworld books have become darker they really mean the series is growing up. In 'The Colour of Magic' most of the city is set alight. It's a joke, in much the same way that the Earth is destroyed almost at the start of Douglas Adams's 'The Hitchhikers Guide to the Galaxy.'

Terry Pratchett

Books are those faithful mirrors that reflect to our mind the minds of sages and heroes.

Edward Gibbon

Students do everything on laptops these days, so I

definitely think electronic books are a trend that's going to expand.

Steven Pinker

Every child's taste is different. Don't worry if they're not reading 'War and Peace' at age 12. First, build a good foundation and a positive attitude about reading by letting them pick the stories they enjoy. Make friends with a bookseller or librarian. They are a wealth of information on finding books that kids enjoy.

Rick Riordan

Works of art often last forever, or nearly so. But exhibitions themselves, especially gallery exhibitions, are like flowers; they bloom and then they die, then exist only as memories, or pressed in magazines and books.

Jerry Saltz

All summer, I read fiction because you must read for the pleasure and beauty of it, and not only for research. I don't read thrillers, romance or mystery, and I don't read self-help books because I don't believe in shortcuts and loopholes.

Isabel Allende

When I was a kid, I was a bit of a space geek. I loved the space program and all things NASA. I would read books about our solar system; I had pictures of the Space Shuttle on my bedroom wall. And yes, I even went to Space Camp.

Simon Sinek

I demand that my books be judged with utmost severity, by knowledgeable people who know the rules of grammar and of logic, and who will seek beneath the footsteps of my commas the lice of my thought in the head of my style.

Louis Aragon

Books were my window on the world. Growing up at the Elephant and Castle, which was very rough, my paradise was the library.

Michael Caine

So he said 'I'm going to chop off the bottom of one of your trouser legs and put it in a library.' I thought 'That's a turn-up for the books.'

Tommy Cooper

www.ingramcontent.com/pod-product-compliance
Lightning Source LLC
Chambersburg PA
CBHW070636290526
45790CB00001B/116